SQUADRO

NO. 56

THE HAWKER
TYPHOON
- THE CANADIAN SQUADRONS -

PHIL H. LISTEMANN

ISBN: 979-1096490-96-7

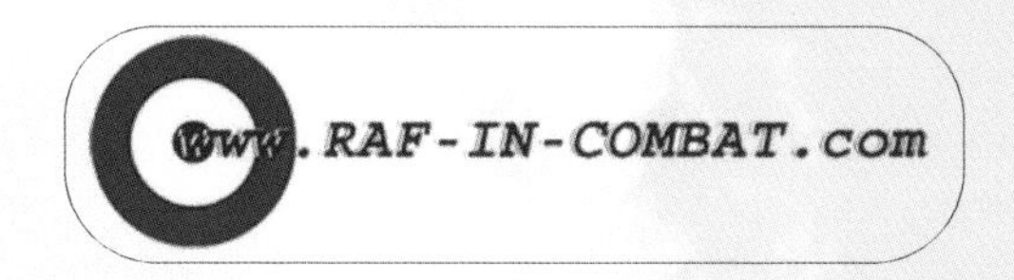

Colour profiles: Chris Thomas

Special thanks to Chris Thomas for his contribution

Glossary of Terms

Personel :

(aus)/RAF: Australian serving in the RAF
(bel)/RAF: Belgian serving in the RAF
(can)/RAF: Canadian serving in the RAF
(cz)/RAF: Czechoslovak serving in the RAF
(nfl)/RAF: Newfoundlander serving in the RAF
(nl)/RAF: Dutch serving in the RAF
(nz)/RAF: New Zealander serving in the RAF
(pol)/RAF: Pole serving in the RAF
(rho)/RAF: Rhodesian serving in the RAF
(sa)/RAF: South African serving in the RAF
(us)/RAF - RCAF : American serving in the RAF or RCAF

Ranks

G/C : Group Captain
W/C : Wing Commander
S/L : Squadron Leader
F/L : Flight Lieutenant
F/O : Flying Officer
P/O : Pilot Officer
W/O : Warrant Officer
F/Sgt : Flight Sergeant
Sgt : Sergeant
Cpl : Corporal
LAC : Leading Aircraftman

Other

ATA: Air Transport Auxiliary
CO : Commander
DFC : Distinguished Flying Cross
DFM : Distinguished Flying Medal
DSO : Distinguished Service Order
Eva. : Evaded
ORB : Operational Record Book
OTU : Operational Training Unit
PoW : Prisoner of War
PAF: Polish Air Force
RAF : Royal Air Force
RAAF : Royal Australian Air Force
RCAF : Royal Canadian Air Force
RNZAF : Royal New Zealand Air Force
SAAF : South African Air Force
s/d: Shot down
Sqn : Squadron
† : Killed

Codenames - Offensive Operations - Fighter Command

Circus:
Bombers heavily escorted by fighters, the purpose being to bring enemy figthers into combat.

Ramrod:
Bombers escorted by fighters, the primary aim being to destroy a target.

Ranger:
Large formation freelance intrusion over enemy territory with aim of wearing down enemy figthers.

Rhubard:
Freelance fighter sortie against targets of opportunity.

Roadstead:
Dive bombing and low level attacks on enemy ships at sea or in harbour

Rodeo:
A fighter sweep without bombers.

Sweep:
An offensive flight by fighters designed to draw up and clear the enemy from the sky.

The Hawker Typhoon

The Hawker Typhoon was designed to Air Ministry specification F.18/37 which sought to take advantage of the new generation of 2000hp engines and satisfy the latest requirements in armament. This major step up demanded a larger and more advanced airframe than that of the company's then current Hurricane and by March 1938 work had commenced on the first two prototypes; one with the Napier Sabre, soon called 'Typhoon' (P5212) and the other with a Rolls-Royce Vulture, later to be named the 'Tornado' (P5219); this latter machine was the first to fly, on 6 October 1939. The Vulture did not give too many problems in the Hawker fighter but by the end of 1940 it was experiencing serious trouble with its installation in the Avro Manchester bomber, and as a result the project was abandoned. With the third engine (Bristol Centaurus) of the new generation still some way off, the Air Ministry had little option but to concentrate on the Typhoon, which had made its first flight on 24 February 1940. The new aircraft encountered teething problems and was also delayed by production priorities for other Hawker types during the Battle of Britain. In accordance with the original specification, the Typhoon was initially armed with no less than twelve 0.303-inch Browning machine guns, the conventional RAF weapon of the time. The wing had been designed with the strength and space to accommodate 20mm cannon, so when this weapon found favour with the Air Ministry, early in 1941, the second prototype Typhoon (P5216) was fitted with two in each wing. This would become the standard Typhoon fixed armament but, due to limited availability of the cannon, the first 73 Typhoons (designated Mk IA) had 12 machine guns before the first cannon-armed versions (Mk IB) came off the line. A further 37 Mk IAs were built, scattered among the early Mk IBs.

During its early operational life the Typhoon had to overcome problems that threatened to end its service, notably carbon monoxide ingress, structural failure and an unreliable powerplant. The major issue of the tail structure failing in flight due to flutter-induced fatigue, caused at least 25 accidents and the death of 23 pilots, but was eventually remedied so that, by the last quarter of 1943, the Typhoon had become a reliable aircraft. Improvements included the introduction of the new single piece 'blown' hood, a four-bladed propeller and an enlarged tailplane, but there was no change in designation. When production ceased in November 1945, 3317 Typhoons had been built.

Operational service

The Hawker Typhoon was rushed into service with No 56 Squadron in late 1941. There were great hopes the new fighter could counter the latest German threat, the Fw 190, and its dominance over the Spitfire Mk.V, the then backbone of Fighter Command. The introduction into service was plagued by many accidents, mainly due to engine failures, but by July 1942 the tail unit failure, as mentioned earlier, had become a major concern. For more than a year the Typhoon's future was jeopardised by this issue, the unreliable Sabre engine and disappointing performance (primarily at high altitude), including a poor rate of climb. The aircraft, however, was

The evolution of the Typhoon is illustrated in the photographs below. Typhoon IA R7579, the fourth production aircraft built by Gloster (who built all but 17 of the 3317 total) in flight; the long rectangular patches on the leading edges of the wing obscure the muzzles of 6 machine guns on each side. The poor view to the rear soon attracted heavy criticism, leading to a series of improvements. *(CT Collection)*

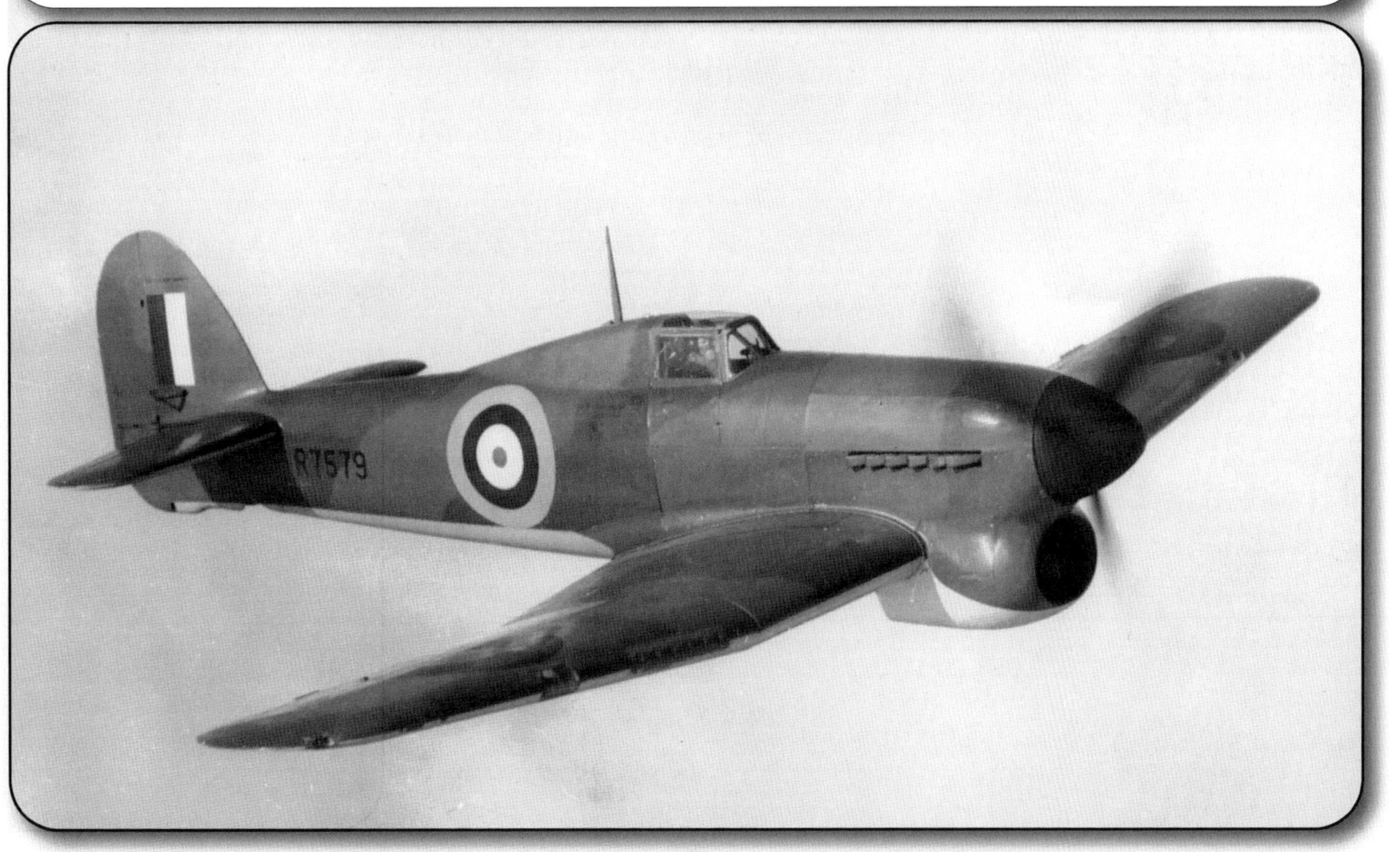

Gloster-built Typhoon R7646 spent two and a half years on development trials with Hawker and A&AEE and is seen here with the trial installation for the first major canopy improvement. The armament has been upgraded to IB standard for trials and would later be used for gun-heating, 250/500lb bomb trials and development of a tropical radiator. *(CT Collection)*

very fast at low altitude and managed to counter the low and fast German fighter-bombers which had begun attacking the English coastal towns in late 1942, claiming at least 57, including 42 of the much-vaunted Fw 190s. By the time the initial engine and tail unit problems were solved, therefore, the Typhoon had found the role in which it would excel, low level interception, and, later, close support armed with bombs or rockets. It was duly chosen as the 2nd TAF's prime fighter-bomber for the forth-coming invasion of NW Europe. From the last quarter of 1942 onwards, the number of Typhoon squadrons increased considerably, re-equipping existing Hurricane squadrons or forming new units.

At first pure fighters were produced, but, by the spring of 1943, only the fighter-bomber version was coming off the production line and by the end of the year all the Typhoon squadrons were undertaking some form of ground attack role. On the eve of D-Day the Typhoon had become the backbone of the 2TAF fighter-bomber force with no less than eighteen squadrons active. A dozen of these were equipped with the latest RAF weapon, the Rocket Projectile (RP), as were two more, still with ADGB, that were positioned to defend either end of the Channel. The success of the RP in Normandy and the following campaign was largely due to the excellent platform the Typhoon provided with its strong wing and inherent stability. Spitfire variants available in 1943-1944 could not carry the RP weapon and Mustangs, with their long range, were required for other roles. The Typhoon was rapidly phased out when the war ended as the RAF had more than enough of the Typhoon's successor, the Hawker Tempest, to fulfill its postwar ground attack requirements. Complex, expensive to service and maintain, no suitable role existed for the Typhoon in peacetime, most were scrapped before the end of 1947.

The sliding blown hood was the ultimate solution to the rear view problem and was much-copied on other types. Also visible on MN686 is the larger tailplane (note it overlaps the pre-painted rear fuselage band) and a 4-blade propeller. Although some more than half (c.1750) of the Typhoons were built with the earlier canopy, some 500 were subsequently rebuilt with the sliding hood. *(CT Collection)*

The final stage came when the Typhoon became a fighter-bomber. At first bombs were carried under the wings (a 500 or 1000 pounder under each wing). Later on, unguided air-to-ground rockets were installed, with four under each wing, making the Typhoon an excellent close support fighter. By 1944, with 2TAF, the Typhoon squadrons were either equipped with bombs or rockets.
(CT Collection)

Each Airfield/Wing of 2TAF had an Officer Commanding, a wing commander position (later changed to group captain in July 1944), and a wing leader responsible for leading the wing in combat. No. 143 (RCAF) Wing was formed on 10 January 1944 as 143 (RCAF) Airfield (changed to 143 Wing in May) to control the three Canadian Typhoon squadrons - 438, 439 & 440 - and had three OCs. Top left: W/C Frank W. Hillock, a pre-war RCAF Auxiliary officer who served with 1 Sqn (RCAF) during the Battle of Britain. In January 1941, he switched to the night fighter role in joining 406 (RCAF) Sqn as a flight commander. Then, between August 1942 and May 1943, he took command of another night fighter unit, 410 (RCAF), to complete his first tour. In January 1944, to start his second tour, he assumed command of 143 Airfield/Wing, a position he left in July, replaced by Group Captain Paul Y. Davoud (DSO, DFC). The latter (top right) was a pre-war graduate of the Royal Military College, serving with the RAF until 1935 before flying as a commercial pilot until July 1940 when he joined the RCAF. Because of his huge flying experience, he at first served as a flying instructor before being posted overseas to 410 (RCAF) Sqn as CO. In September, he left to command 409 (RCAF), another night fighter squadron, until February 1943 when he was injured in a Beaufighter crash. On recovery in June, he was posted to command 418 (RCAF) Sqn, a night intruder unit, and led it until January 1944 when he was rested. In July 1944, he was back on the front line and took command of 143 Wing. In January 1945, he relinquished command to another regular RCAF officer, G/C Arthur D. Nesbitt (DFC), a Battle of Britain veteran with 1 Sqn RCAF who eventually commanded that unit (renamed 401 Sqn) between March and September 1941 before he was repatriated home. In Canada, Nesbitt was given command of 111 Sqn which he left in June 1942 to take various non-operational positions as a wing commander. Sent overseas again in March 1944, he first commanded 144 (RCAF) Wing until the disbandment of that unit in July 1944. After a stay with 83 Group HQ, he commanded 143 Wing from January 1945 until the end of the war.

January 1944 August 1945

Victories - confirmed or probable claims: 1.0

First operational sortie:
20.03.44
Last operational sortie:
04.05.45

Number of sorties: *ca.* **4,000**

Total aircraft written-off: 44

Aircraft lost on operations: 39
Aircraft lost in accidents: 5

Squadron code letters:

F3

Commanding Officers

S/L Frank G. Grant	Can./ J.5056	RCAF	18.11.43	28.07.44
S/L Jack R. Beirnes	Can./ C.13458	RCAF	28.07.44	13.10.44
S/L Ross F. Reid	Can./ J.9936	RCAF	13.10.44	29.12.44
F/L Peter Wilson *(†)*	Can./ J.9876	RCAF	29.12.44	01.01.45
S/L Ross F. Reid	Can./ J.9936	RCAF	01.01.45	20.01.45
S/L James E. Hogg *(†)*	Can./ J.2119	RCAF	20.01.45	23.03.45
S/L Jack R. Beirnes *(†)*	Can./ C.13458	RCAF	06.04.45	01.06.45
S/L Paul Bissky	Can./ J.5833	RCAF	04.06.45	26.08.45

Squadron Usage

Originally No. 118 Squadron RCAF based in Canada, initially as a bomber-reconnaissance unit with Westland Lysanders, but later as a fighter unit with Grumman Goblins based near Montreal (see *SQUADRONS! No. 9*), the squadron converted to Curtiss P-40 Kittyhawks and was based in Alaska and British Columbia until 1943 for air defence duties in case of Japanese attacks. Selected to be sent overseas to reinforce the Second Tactical Air Force (2TAF) and participate in the invasion of Europe, the unit arrived in the UK on 15 November 1943 under the command of S/L F.G. Grant, a long-serving member of the unit, and was renumbered No. 438 (RCAF) Squadron on the 18th. The squadron was based at Digby and received Hurricane Mk.IVs for ground-attack duties upon joining No. 143 Airfield in January 1944 when the latter was formed on the 10th. The squadron soon moved to Ayr with its full com-

Succeeding S/L Grant (see bio at the end of the book), the first 438 CO, Jack Beirnes, a Canadian from Manitoba, initially tried to enlist as a motor mechanic in 1934 but was rejected. He tried twice more to enlist in the RAF, in 1935 and 1937, but did not succeed. In April 1940, he finally managed to join the RCAF. However, once his training was completed, he served in Canada as a staff pilot and then joined an operational unit, 118 Sqn RCAF, in December 1941 as an NCO. He was commissioned in July 1942. In October 1943, he was posted overseas with the unit, which became No. 438 (RCAF) Squadron upon arrival in the UK and converted to Typhoons. Beirnes was one of the two flight commanders. He participated in many ops with 438 and eventually assumed command in July 1944. In October, his tour ended and he was repatriated to Canada. A DFC was awarded at the same time. In March 1945, Beirnes was sent back to the UK and returned to 438 as OC once more. He led the squadron until the end of the war. Soon after, however, on 1 June 1945, he was killed in a flying accident.

Pilots of 438 Squadron in the early stages of training on Hurricanes in January 1944:
Front: Flying Officers N.E. Dawber and R.H. Burden, and Sgt W.H. Morrison, the only NCO pilot of the squadron at the time (†15.08.44).
Next row: Flying Officers HG Upham, R.E. Coffey († 30.07.45 in a road accident as CO 440 Sqn), VE McMann (PoW 18.10.44), J.C.W. Hope († in a flying accident in a Hurricane, 14.01.44), T.A. Bugg (†12.08.44), and G.A. Edington (PoW 18.08.44), Flight Lieutenants J.R. Beirnes (†01.06.45) and P. Wilson (†01.01.45), and Flying Officers R.M. McKenzie (†18.07.44) and L.E. Park (USA, †27.06.44).
On the wing: Flying Officers J.E. Cornelison (USA, †29.09.44), D.W. Banting and A.B. Newsome (†20.07.44), and F/L R.F. Reid.
The four behind are Flying Officers R.E. Johnson (†15.07.44 during an artillery strike), A.C. Brooker, R.C. Getty and J.E. Hilton.

plement of aircraft. Conversion to the Typhoon got underway almost immediately, three being on strength at the end of the month. In February, training continued but only four more Typhoons were taken on charge and the bulk of flying was still done by the Hurricanes (362 hours against 71). On 18 March, the squadron was re-located at Hurn with its mixed fleet. Two days later, under the leadership of the wing leader, W/C R.T.P. Davidson, 438 had the privilege of carrying out the first operation by a 143 Airfield unit, and, of course, the first for the squadron, with a fighter sweep to the aerodrome of Cherbourg–Alderney. Participating in the sweep with the wing leader were Grant and his two flight commanders, Flight Lieutenants J.R. Beirnes and P. Wilson. After this symbolic entry into the European war, the squadron had to wait until the 30th to return to action. On that day, and the following one, two uneventful sweeps of ten Typhoons each were carried out.
The stay at Hurn was short and a move was made to Furnington on 3 April. Now the squadron was fully equipped with Typhoons and 438, with the wing, or part of it, was regularly involved in sweeps over Occupied Europe. Initially, Noball operations (against V-1 sites) were carried out; 84 sorties were flown in April and no losses sustained even though several Typhoons were hit by flak. In May, the squadron suffered its first loss. That day, W/C Davidson was scheduled to lead a sweep to the Douai marshalling yards. The day started badly for him as his regular mount became unserviceable and he had to fly one of 438's Typhoons. For reasons unknown, during the attack, the engine of the Typhoon failed and Davidson was obliged to make a forced landing near Bethune. Happily, he managed to evade capture and eventually joined the French Resistance; he was liberated in September. His position was taken by W/C M.T. Judd soon after his loss. Ops continued until the 22nd when the squadron was sent to Hutton Cranswick for an armament practice camp from the 23rd, being sent back to Hurn four days later; operations resumed at once. May was not as intense as it could have been with only 135 sorties carried out. In June, the days before D-Day, three sweeps were flown on the 2nd, 3rd and 5th. June 6, D-Day, involved three sweeps for 438, at 06.55, 17.15 and 20.50, in support of the landings. Various ground targets were attacked and destroyed; all aircraft returned to base safely. Over the following week, a high number of sorties were understandably carried out; 438 seems to have held on to its luck, at least until the 12th, when the first loss was recorded. That day, ops did not start until noon. Eight Typhoons, with two others acting as top cover, took off at 12.15 for a dive-bombing op. The tar-

All three Canadian Typhoon squadrons remained equipped for bombing throughout their existence. Here, some 1,000-lb bombs are waiting to be fitted under Typhoon MN426/F3-H which was usually flown during the summer of 1944 by the CO, S/L F.G. Grant, who finished his tour at the end of July 1944. *(CT Collection)*

get was a forested area near Vandes. Bombing was good though results were not seen. On the way back, the Typhoon flown F/O T.A. Bugg began to lose oil pressure rapidly, possibly due to flak damage, and eventually the engine cut out. He managed to ditch the Typhoon properly, a feat in itself due to the radiator, and was seen soon after to climb into his dinghy. Another Typhoon circled until a boat picked him up 15 minutes later. The squadron was called on to carry out another sortie that evening, taking off at 21.35. The op had a bad start as, of the eight fighter-bombers and four escorts 438 put up, one fighter-bomber developed engine trouble before take-off while another had an instrument failure shortly after taking off and turned around accompanied by his No. 2. The misfortune continued, however, and F/L Wilson was apparently hit by flak on the way to target and had to drop out with his wingman. That left seven aircraft in the formation. Wilson was seen to jettison his bombs but was lost sight of at about 2,000 feet, within gliding distance of the nearby emergency landing strip. Luck continued to evade him as news soon reached the squadron that he was in hospital with a broken arm and a gash on his leg. Flak was not the only danger over Normandy. Indeed, four days later, 438 lost another of its own, shot down by a Bf109 near Pont-l'Évêque, when four Typhoons were caught by surprise by eight Bf109s while attacking a railway tunnel. Flying Officer R.C. Getty managed to evade capture and was able to link up with advancing Canadian troops some five weeks later. The squadron came close to losing another pilot on the 25th when a furious dogfight took place between four Typhoons and several Bf109s and Fw190s (no less than 30 were reported!). No claims were made, or losses sustained, even though one aircraft came back badly damaged; F/L J.R. Beirnes was obliged to make a wheels-up landing near Tangmere due to a flat tyre. The luck which had been with 438 so far, in terms of fortunate escapes, left for a moment as, the next day, the squadron experienced its first fatality. Flying Officer L.E. Park, an American from Missouri, who was shot down by flak attacking a ground target. He received a direct hit and his Typhoon was seen to fall in pieces south-west of Caen. Later in the day, the squadron moved to B.9/Lantheuil in France. In all, 438 carried out close to 450 sorties in June, a rather intense period in support of the invasion. Fully engaged now in the Battle of Normandy, the squadron sustained light losses in July and flew 250 sorties, quite a low figure compared to other units. The first loss took place on the 15th and was not flight related. That day, seven pilots on board a truck heading towards a spot near Caen, to pick up lumber for the new parachute truck, were hit by a shell. Flying Officer R.E. Johnson was killed while two other pilots were slightly injured. The next day, three Typhoons from 440 took off led by S/L Gooding with W/O McConevy on his right who left the runway and at some stages hit one 438's Typhoon (MN633) on the wing and one of the 1,000-lbs bomb exploded. McConevy was killed (see 440 part) and two groundcrew from 438, LAC R.H. Wilman and LAC J.S. Holmes were also killed; Typhoon MN633 was repaired. From an operational point of view, 438 sustained its first loss for the month on the 18th. In the early op, an attack on a bridge over the Orne, F/L R.M. McKenzie failed to pull out of his dive and was seen to crash by one of the other pilots. It is believed flak, which was intense and accurate, was responsible for his loss. Two days later, another wing operation led to the loss of another Typhoon. The target was a crossroads at Fontenay-le-Marmion; the 'Tiffies' were armed with 1000-lb bombs. The ceiling was too low, it was raining and the target was covered with heavy cloud. Heavy accu-

rate flak was encountered and, probably due to the low altitude the aircraft were forced to fly, two Typhoons were hit. One aircraft, flown by F/O A.B. Newsome, was hit in the radiator. He stayed with it until the engine cut and, well over Allied lines, he baled out. The other Typhoon, piloted by now F/L Bugg, who had successfully ditched on 12 June, was badly hit in the wing. Bugg managed to maintain control, despite one of the 1000-lb bombs hanging up, and landed at B.6. While more incidents were reported up to the end of the month, no more Typhoons or pilots were lost. A change of command took place, however, with S/L Grant handing over to F/L J.Beirnes (one of the flight commanders he flew the squadron's first op with on 20 March) at the end of the month. While July had been very acceptable regarding losses, some would say light compared to other Typhoon units, August was totally different, the squadron sustaining losses at a level not yet experienced. The list of pilots killed was initiated by F/O D.K. Moores on 3 August when he was killed while diving on his target near Hénonville; he received a direct hit by flak and exploded. He was followed nine days later by Bugg who was killed in similar circumstances near Le Mesnil-Villement. Now deeply involved in the Battle of Falaise, the number of sorties increased to put pressure on the retreating German troops who could still put up a deadly curtain of flak; on 15 August, they indirectly sealed the fate of F/O W.H. Morrison who hit trees trying to avoid flak while attacking METs near Trun. In the same vein, flak was also indirectly responsible for the death of F/O G.H. Sharpe on the 18th. He was not seen to crash but the burning wreckage of his Typhoon was seen on the ground near Orbec. It is believed he made a tight turn at low level, when making his attack, and spun in. However, the same day, flak definitely hit the Typhoon flown by F/L G.P. Edington near Roiville; he had to bale out. He was captured and would have the dubious honour of being the sole survivor of those 438 pilots lost in August. The squadron had lost five Typhoons in a two-week period. These were severe losses, but 438 was spared any more before the end of the month, which saw close to 500 sorties carried out.
At the end of August, the squadron, with the wing, began to make some moves forward. On the 31st, 438 relocated to B.24/Saint-André, on 2 September to B.48/Glisy, and eventually B.58/Melsbroek in Belgium where it would remain for most of September, until the 26th at least, when a final move was made to B.78/Eindhoven, a base 438 would stay at until mid-March 1945. Needless to say, these moves had a negative impact on the rhythm of operations and the number of sorties dropped to 375 for the month. Routine was the word for the first 26 days of September, however, with no major event being recorded. The 27th, though, would be a day to remember. The Allies were deeply involved in Operation Market Garden so air support was crucial. The squadron flew five ops that day, three being low-level bombing attacks (against intercepted trains on the move and at stations), one fighter patrol and a scramble. Five trains were destroyed; good results were scored on each bombing attack. The scramble took place at 16.40 and involved four Typhoons against about 20 or more German fighters. Nothing was seen in the first part of the patrol but, on turning for base ten miles east of Nijmegen, the leader, F/L Newsome, saw enemy aircraft attacking and called a break to the left. As they started to break, F/O H.G. Upham saw about 20 Bf109s coming out of cloud at 4 o'clock and told White 4, W/O A.B. Harle, to break with him to the right. A dogfight ensued and Upham managed to get on a Bf109's tail at about 350 yards. The Bf109 climbed through 4–5 layers of cloud; Upham followed him, firing when he could see him. The Bf109 began to stream black smoke from its engine. At the last burst, Upham saw strikes, a flame about a quarter of the length of the fuselage, and a large puff of black smoke. When he reached this smoke puff, there was a smoke trail heading toward the ground. Upham let down out of cloud to 100 feet and saw about 100 yards of burning debris. The Bf109 was credited as confirmed thanks to the camera gun which was used. Sadly, the claim was balanced the next day with the loss of F/O A.H. Vickers shot down by flak near Papenbeek while attacking trains; he was obliged to bale out and spent the rest of the war as a PoW. The next day, it was the turn of F/O J.E. Cornelison, an American from Kentucky, to be posted missing. While returning from another show, four of 438's Typhoons were caught by 30 or more Bf109s near Nijmegen. The Bf109s clearly had the advantage. Only three Typhoons made their way home, with one more claim, an Fw190 damaged by F/Sgt R.G. Cox after a burst from 400 yards, and it was later learned that Cornelison had been killed in the short, but intense engagement. With autumn slowly arriving over Europe, the number of sorties decreased until the end of the year, with 360 carried out in October, 240 in November and 205 in December. Of the three Canadian squadrons, 438 remained the 'Lucky Squadron' within the wing, having lost just six Typhoons over the previous three months. In detail, in October, F/L Newsome, the A Flight CO was shot down on the 7th while dive bombing a target south of Coesfeld in Germany; he plunged directly into the ground and explo-

S/L Beirnes taxiing out in his Typhoon, coded F3-B, at Eindhoven at the end of the summer of 1944. The letter 'B' was what he used for his aircraft, including the Typhoon in which he was killed in June 1945. *(CT Collection)*

ded. More fortunate was F/L V.E. McMann, at dawn on the 18th, when his engine cut before reaching the target on the first operation of the day. He tried to glide back, using the engine sparingly, but was unable to make the Allied lines. He eventually made a forced landing three miles south of Rheden and was captured. October also saw S/L Beirnes relinquish command to S/L R.F. Reid on the 13th. On 6 November, four dive-bombing ops were performed; all were successful. Besides that, a Typhoon flown by F/O R.G. Crosby was lost when its engine cut during a morning recce due to a fractured sleeve valve. Crosby made a safe landing two miles from the aerodrome and was able to escape unscathed before the Typhoon caught fire. Ten days later, F/O N.E. Dawber was the second and final loss for November. He was hit by flak near Arnhem during the last op of the day. He managed to bale out over Allied lines and was retrieved by British troops, making it back to the squadron within a couple of hours. The first three-and-a-half weeks of December confirmed the squadron's 'lucky' reputation, but 438 was hit badly on Christmas Eve with two Typhoons and their pilots, W/O R.F. Breen and F/O D.J. Washburn, shot down and killed by flak while strafing during an armed recce in the Malmedy–Emskirchen–Mayen–Houfflalize sector. Obviously, these two losses dramatically dampened Christmas spirit the next day. The squadron also lost another pilot on the 30th but not in combat; S/L Reid who, being tour expired upon reaching 100 operational sorties, was replaced by S/L P.Wilson, one of the original flight commanders who had been shot down and injured on 12 June. The squadron's luck seemed to have run out in January 1945. B.78/Eindhoven was the first airfield to be hit by the Luftwaffe during its Operation *Bodenplatte*. The airfield was attacked by JG 3 and the German flyers obtained one of their best results of the entire day. When the attack began, 16 Typhoons, eight each from Nos. 438 and 440 Squadrons, were waiting for take-off. The 438 aircraft had entered the runway and two were already on their take-off run, including the new CO. He apparently throttled back, pulled over at the end of the runway and got out of his aircraft, wounded in the stomach; he died a few minutes later. The other Typhoon, flown by F/O R.W. Keller, managed to get airborne, but he was at once shot down and killed. For the other pilots still waiting to take off, they were strafed but extraordinarily lucky. Temporary F/O D. Campbell could not get out of his aircraft during the strafing run so crouched down throughout the whole action even as his machine suffered several hits. The other five pilots – Flying Officers Frank R.F. Skelly, W.L. Beatty and J.A. Lord, and P/O A.B. Harle and F/L F.X.J. Regan – managed to get out of their Typhoons and escape being hit. A couple found a slit trench nearby while others hid behind a small pile of sand. Of the remaining Typhoons waiting for take-off, all were damaged by the strafing, three badly enough that they were struck off charge soon after. Despite this setback, 438 was back on duty the next day for an armed recce. Command was temporarily given back to S/L Reid, he was still grounded, until a new CO was appointed. The squadron continued to carry out ops despite unfavorable conditions, but no losses were recorded until the 20th. It was a nice and bright day, ideal for carrying out support sorties. Returning from a bombing sortie, F/L Edmund J.D. McKay's engine cut out in the circuit and he was obliged to make a wheels-up landing which proved fatal for the Typhoon. The clear weather also meant the flak gunners would have perfect visibility to deliver accurate fire and that is exactly what they did over the next few days. On the 21st, a ground collision while taxiing cut F/O P.G. Mackem's Typhoon in two; he miraculously escaped unscathed. The other Typhoon, with F/L A.A. MacDonald at the controls, was badly damaged but repairable. The bad run continued for the next two days with Frank Skelly, who survived the 1 January strafing attacks, being seen to explode in flames and spiral down near the target. On the 23rd, the next day, F/O I.J.V. Wallace was lost in the same circumstances. He was hit when about to release his bombs, raising concerns regarding the bomb-release system and leading to an investigation by the Armament Officer. This point was one of priority for the new CO, S/L J.E. Hogg, having officially taken over on the 23rd (he had arrived a few days earlier); fortunately for him, there were no more losses before the end of the month. In all, close to 200 sorties were flown in January and this increased to 340 in February. After a disastrous January, February reverted to the low loss rate to which 438 was quite happily accustomed. Only two Typhoons were lost in February. The 14th was one of the most favourable days for flying since the beginning of the month and 438 worked hard with only a short break for lunch. Flying Officer F.A. Nixon, one of the newer pilots, did not make it to lunch. He was believed to have been hit by flak near Geldern while attacking a train on the

Typhoon F3-P under repair at No. 419 Repair & Salvage Unit. While 438 had a low loss rate during the Battle of Normandy, many aircraft were hit by flak, sometimes severely.

Groundcrew at work servicing MN716/F3-A at Eidhoven in October 1944. *(CT Collection)*

first strike of the day. He was not seen to bale out due to glare from the bright sun, but news was later received that he was safe in German hands. A few days later, the squadron sent off eight Typhoons as part of a wing attack on V-1 sites near Piershil in Holland. The attack was very successful, as all the bombs fell in the target area and explosions were seen, but W/O2 G.R. Errington was hit by flak and soon started to stream glycol. No message was heard from him before he was seen to bale out and float toward earth, directly into captivity. Another pilot was shot down and captured on 2 March. While attacking marshalling yards near Dulmen, F/L Donald J. Heard was hit by the area's intense flak barrage. His aircraft was seen to zoom steeply out of the bomb dive on fire. After gaining considerable height, the tail assembly broke off and the Typhoon dived into the ground. Despite appearances, Heard managed to evacuate his aircraft and saw out the war as a PoW. The squadron then moved back to England to undertake an armament practice camp at Warmwell. The camp lasted until 2 April when the squadron moved back to the Continent. This was done without the CO, S/L Hogg, who was killed during a practice dive-bombing flight on the 23rd. He was seen to crash into the Channel while pulling out of a dive off Portland. What happened could not be determined, but it was believed he had fallen victim to a high-speed stall. The stay at Warmwell was also marked by another accident when, while conducting a flight test in preparation for the move to the Continent the next day, W/O W.J. Kinsella experienced an engine failure and made a forced landing at Warmwell; he emerged unhurt, but the Typhoon was written off.

The new station was B.100/Goth in Germany where the wing had been based since the end of March. The squadron arrived on 3 April and the first armed recce, led by F/L R.H. Burlen, was flown that evening. The operational restart was tough for the Canadians as they suffered two losses the following

When S/L Beirnes became tour expired in October, he was replaced by Ross Reid, who was also close to the end of his tour. At the time, he was one of the flight commanders. He had previously served in Canada with 14 Sqn RCAF in British Columbia flying Kittyhawks for a short time before being transferred to 118 Sqn RCAF in the spring of 1942. When he left 438, he was the longest-serving wartime pilot with a single unit, having spent 32 months with 118/438. A DFC was awarded in February 1945. He was repatriated in April 1945 before being released from service in August.

Some of the pilots of 438 in mid-January 1945.
On the Typhoon: unknown, F/O R.E. Oldfin, F/L E.J.D. McKay, and Flying Officers J.P. Dewar, F.R.F. Skelly (†22.01.45), J.A. Lord, A.C Richards, W.L. Beatty and R.C. Getty.
Front: F/O D.V. Campbell, F/L A.C. Brooker, P/O R.G. Fox, S/L R.F. Reid (on temporary duty but grounded having reached the 100-sortie mark), F/L R.E. Spooner, F/O I.J.V. Wallace (†23.01.45), W/O2 W.J. Kinsella (†04.04.45), F/L E.J. McAlpine (†04.04.45), P/O A.B. Harle and F/O G.R. Errington (PoW 21.02.45).

day. On the last armed recce of the day, carried out in the evening at around 19.00, four Typhoons, led once more by Burlen, were jumped by a dozen Bf109s; only two 438 pilots returned from this unbalanced engagement. Flight Lieutenant E.J. McAlpine and the unfortunate W/O Kinsella lost their lives. Two days later, the squadron welcomed S/L Beirnes back. He was posted in for another tour of command following his stint the previous summer and autumn. The job waiting for him was considerable as no less than 600 sorties were flown in April, despite two moves during the month: B.110/Osnabrück on the 12th, and then B150/Hustedt on the 21st. Beirnes had to manage the inevitable losses that came with such a period of intense activity. On the 14th, F/O J.G.S.J. Livingstone, while in the circuit returning from a successful sortie, suddenly flicked over and spun into the ground. No cause was determined and his death remained unexplained. Two days later, possibly hit by flak while attacking railway targets near Wümme, F/O J.K. Brown had his engine cut and, a few seconds later, had to bale out. It was later discovered he had become a PoW. On the 23rd, P/O T. Hartnett, an Irishman educated in Canada, was posted missing after he was seen entering cloud south-west of Lüneberg. Two days later, F/O T.M. Jones was shot down; he was captured but only briefly imprisoned. He was hit by flak south-east off Bovenau during a strafing attack and pulled up to approximatively 2,000 feet before the Typhoon spiralled into the ground. The squadron's last loss of the month, and the war, took place the next day when F/O E.D. Brydon, a newcomer, hit trees and crashed during a low-level attack south-west of Gnissau. The squadron carried out what proved to be its final ops on 4 May when eight Typhoons, armed with two 500-lb bombs each, flew an anti-shipping strike and attacked a 1,000-ton vessel. No bombs hit the ship, but it was duly strafed. In just four days in May, 123 sorties were flown. The Allies remained vigilant in the early days of peace following the German surrender; a training programme was soon established to maintain a certain level of skill among the pilots. While the wartime 'Lucky Squadron' moniker had stuck during its time in combat, the squadron lost its reputation in the weeks fol-

James Hogg officially took over 438 on 20 January 1945. He enlisted in the RCAF before the war as groundcrew but, in March 1942, was accepted to undertake a pilot course and, at the end of the year, was posted to 123 Sqn, in Canada, which was sent to the UK during the autumn of 1943. On 31 December 1943, this squadron became 439 Sqn and Hogg completed a full tour with it in November 1944. A DFC followed in January 1945. His was rested until called to lead 438 Sqn and was in this role when he was killed in a flying accident on 23 March 1945.

lowing the cessation of hostilities. On 14 May, while on a wing display, Sgt Arthur G. Wilks, while switching from his long-range tanks at about 400 feet, suffered a leak in the lines and was forced to land at B.166. He took off again very shortly afterwards but, when at about 500 feet, his engine cut again and he was forced to make an emergency belly landing. He escaped unhurt and the aircraft was scheduled for repair but, with the end of the war in Europe and the type being stricken from the RAF's inventory, this never happened. On 29 May, another move was made, the squadron going with the wing to B.166/Flensburg. The ferry ended badly for F/Sgt R.S. Guerd. He overshot the runway and, in doing so, lost power and crashed, sealing the fate of the Typhoon. A dramatic accident took place three days later when, shortly after take-off and just a few miles within Denmark, the CO informed the flight his engine was packing up and that he was going down for a forced landing. For some reason, a wingtip touched the ground first and the aircraft broke up, instantly killing S/L Beirnes. He was replaced on 4 June by S/L P. Bissky who would command the unit until its disbandment on 26 August. No major events occurred during this period of time.

Below, Typhoon JR336/F3-X seen just after the German surrender with the 'fishplates', fixed to reinforce the tailplane, clearly visible in white with red outlines. *(CT Collection)*

Claims - 438 Squadron (Confirmed and Probable)

Date	*Pilot*	*SN*	*Origin*	*Type*	*Serial*	*Code*	*Nb*	*Cat.*
27.09.44	F/O Harry G. **Upham**	Can./ J.13455	RCAF	Bf109	**PD476**	F3-E	1.0	C
		Total: 1.0						

Summary of the aircraft lost on Operations - 438 Squadron

Date	Pilot	S/N	Origin	Serial	Code	Fate
08.05.44	W/C Robert T.P. **Davidson**	RAF No. 39968	(CAN)/RAF	**MM957**	F3-N	**Eva.**
12.06.44	F/L Peter **Wilson**	Can./ J.9876	RCAF	**MN346**	F3-X	-
	F/O Theodore A. **Bugg**	Can./ J.11316	RCAF	**MN538**	F3-N	-
16.06.44	F/O Ronald C. **Getty**	Can./ J.27741	RCAF	**MN298**	F3-A	-
27.06.44	F/O Lewis E. **Park**	Can./ J.12491	(US)/RCAF	**MN746**	F3-X	†
18.07.44	F/L Robert M. **McKenzie**	Can./ J.11317	RCAF	**MN707**	F3-E	†
20.07.44	F/O Albert B. **Newsome**	Can./ J.10652	RCAF	**n/k**	F3-F	-
03.08.44	F/O Douglas K. **Moores**	Can./ J.17649	RCAF	**MN321**	F3-G	†
12.08.44	F/L Theodore A. **Bugg**	Can./ J.11316	RCAF	**MN687**	F3-S	†
15.08.44	F/O William H. **Morrison**	Can./ J.27387	RCAF	**MN426**	F3-H	†
18.08.44	F/O George H. **Sharpe**	Can./ J.13612	RCAF	**MN347**	F3-Z	†
	F/L Gordon R. **Edington**	Can./ J.11044	RCAF	**MN579**	F3-J	**PoW**
28.09.44	F/O Albert H. **Vickers**	Can./ J.21585	RCAF	**JR497**	F3-F	**PoW**
29.09.44	F/O John E. **Cornelison**	Can./ J.27764	(US)/RCAF	**PD479**	F3-Q	†
07.10.44	F/L Albert B. **Newsome**	Can./ J.10652	RCAF	**MP135**	F3-G	†
18.10.44	F/O Victor E. **McMann**	Can./ J.13598	RCAF	**MN555**	F3-Z	**PoW**
06.11.44	F/O Robert G. **Crosby**	Can./ C.22655	RCAF	**PD475**	F3-G	**Inj.**
18.11.44	F/O Norman E. **Dawber**	Can./ J.26435	RCAF	**MP131**	F3-J	-
24.12.44	W/O1 Roy F. **Breen**	Can./ R.98134	RCAF	**MP178**	F3-H	†
	F/O Dean J. **Washburn**	Can./ J.29339	RCAF	**MP186**	F3-V	†
01.01.45	F/O Ross W. **Keller**	Can./ J.37649	RCAF	**PD550**	F3-R	†
	F/L Peter **Wilson**	Can./ J.9876	RCAF	**PD556**	F3-Q	†
	destroyed in air raid	-	-	**MN607**	F3-G	-
	destroyed in air raid	-	-	**MN816**	F3-Y	-
	destroyed in air raid	-	-	**MP177**	F3-F	-
20.01.45	F/L Edmund J.D. **McKay**	Can./ J.20030	RCAF	**PD446**	F3-Z	-
21.01.45	F/O Philip G. **Macklem**	Can./ J.24410	RCAF	**RB397**		-
22.01.45	F/O Frank R.F. **Skelly**	Can./ J.35985	RCAF	**MP128**	F3-X	†
23.01.45	F/O Ivan J.V. **Wallace**	Can./ J.29904	RCAF	**RB333**	F3-R	†
14.02.45	F/O Finley A. **Nixon**	Can./ J.35861	RCAF	**RB226**	F3-H	-
21.02.45	W/O2 Gordon R. **Errington**	Can./ R.90970	RCAF	**PD476**	F3-E	**PoW**
02.03.45	F/L Donald J. **Heard**	Can./ J.22976	RCAF	**RB285**	F3-Z	**PoW**
04.04.45	W/O2 William J. **Kinsella**	Can./ R.188931	RCAF	**MP181**	F3-F	†
	F/L Earl J. **McAlpine**	Can./ J.5788	RCAF	**RB217**	F3-J	†
14.04.45	F/O John G.S.J. **Livingstone**	Can./ J.85932	RCAF	**MM989**	F3-R	†
16.04.45	F/O John K. **Brown**	Can./ J.21136	RCAF	**MP192**	F3-J	**PoW**
23.04.45	P/O Timothy **Hartnett**	Can./ J.91195	(IRE)/RCAF	**RB342**	F3-Q	†
25.04.45	F/O Tom M. **Jones**	Can./ J.44192	RCAF	**RB323**	F3-V	**PoW**
26.04.45	F/O Edward D. **Brydon**	Can./ J.44042	RCAF	**RB429**	F3-X	†

Total: 39

Summary of the aircraft lost by accident - 438 Squadron

Date	*Pilot*	*S/N*	*Origin*	*Serial*	*Code*	*Fate*
23.03.45	S/L James E. **Hogg**	Can./ J.21119	RCAF	**MP138**		†
02.04.45	W/O2 William J. **Kinsella**	Can./ R.188931	RCAF	**MN758**	F3-M	-
14.05.45	Sgt Arthur G. **Wilks**	Can./ R.211126	RCAF	**RB466**		-
29.05.45	F/Sgt Robert S. **Guerd**	Can./ R.219163	RCAF	**MN325**		-
01.06.45	S/L Jack R. **Beirnes**	Can./ C.13458	RCAF	**SW393**	F3-B	†

Total: 5

Some 438 pilots who did not make it. Top left, Pete Wilson was promoted to lead 438 on 30 December 1944 but was killed two days later during Operation *Bodenplatte*. He was a long-serving member of 118/438. Bottom: 438's last two wartime casualties. Left, Ted Brydon from Ontario and, right, Timothy Hartnett, an Irishman who had moved to Canada before the war to receive a higher education.

January 1944 August 1945

Victories - confirmed or probable claims: 11.00

First operational sortie: 27.03.44
Last operational sortie: 04.05.45

Number of sorties: *ca.* **4,000**

Total aircraft written-off: 58

Aircraft lost on operations: 50
Aircraft lost in accidents: 8

Squadron code letters:

5V

Commanding Officers

S/L William M. Smith	Can./ C.923	RCAF	31.12.43	09.03.44
S/L Hugues H. Norsworthy	Can./ J.5114	RCAF	09.03.44	12.09.44
S/L Kenneth J. Fiset	Can./ J.9078	RCAF	12.09.44	08.12.44
S/L Robert G. Crosby *(s/d)*	Can./ C.22655	RCAF	08.12.44	22.01.45
S/L James H. Beatty	Can./ J.14471	RCAF	25.01.45	26.08.45

Squadron Usage

Formed in Canada as No. 123 (Army Co-operation Training) Squadron on 15 January 1941 at Rockliffe, Ottawa, the unit provided training and close support and reconnaissance for Canadian troops, using various aircraft like Lysanders, Goblins, Harvards and Hurricanes, the latter being the only type in use from June 1943. Despite its secondary task, the squadron was selected, in the autumn of 1943, to serve overseas and was eventually redesignated No. 439 (RCAF) Squadron on 1 January 1944 upon its arrival in the UK. Placed under 2TAF control almost immediately, it became part of No. 143 (RCAF) Airfield; it was based at Ayr in Scotland to work up to operational status. The CO was S/L W.M. Smith. To ease the transition, the squadron at first received Hurricane Mk.IVs and trained in the use of rocket projectiles. Typhoons soon arrived, six being taken on charge in a couple of days, and the first soloes were performed in early February. The squadron continued using both Hawker types in the following weeks. As far as the Typhoon was concerned, the first major incident took place on the 17th when one caught fire on the ground and was destroyed. Three

Hugh Norsworthy, from Montreal, was the first CO of 439 to lead the squadron on operations. He enlisted in the RCAF in August 1940 and trained on twin-engine aircraft in Canada. Upon completing his training, he sailed to the UK in May 1941. He went to 54 OTU to become a night fighter pilot and was then posted to 85 Sqn in September 1941 to fly the Douglas Havoc. He made his first claim, a Do217 destroyed and shared with a Royal Navy pilot, on the night of 17/18 January 1942. During the year, he converted to the Mosquito. At the end of January 1943, he was posted to 3 Sqn to fly Hawker Typhoons. His stay was short as, in March, he was sent to the Fighter Interception Unit (FIU) and did not return to the squadron until August. He left again in October and was repatriated to Canada in November. He was sent overseas again in February 1944 and, on arrival in the UK, was posted the following month to command 439. He led this unit through the Battle of Normandy until the end of his tour in September 1944. Norsworthy was repatriated, having received the DFC in September, and released from the RCAF in February 1945.

During the spring of 1944, just before D-Day, two of 439's pilots are seen clow.ning about near JR506/5V-R. Left, F/O J.W Ross and, right, F/O R.O. Moen. A few weeks later, on 15 June, Ross was shot down and became a PoW while Moen was killed in action on 12 August. JR506 survived a few months more before being badly damaged by US P-47s which attacked 439 by mistake on 24 December. The Typhoon was too damaged to consider for repair, but its pilot survived unscathed.
(CT Collection)

days later, F/O E.L. Dixon was killed during a practice flight when he crashed into a hillside near New Cumnock. Training continued for the month, without further incident, as more Typhoons arrived. March saw various events of note. First of all, a new CO was appointed when S/L H.H. Norsworthy arrived on the 10th to replace S/L Smith, who was posted out. A week later, the squadron moved south to Hurn to start operations. Delayed several times, the first operational sorties were eventually carried out on the 27th when eight Typhoons were involved in an unsuccessful wing sweep over the Cherbourg Peninsula. The Wing Commander Flying, W/C Davidson, a Canadian serving in the RAF, flew with 439. Two more sweeps were flown on the 30th and 31st over the same area, but both were unsuccessful. The squadron moved to Funtington on 2 April. It seems it was a not lucky move as, two days later, in the afternoon, P/O A.C. Clarke overturned on landing. He was flying in formation with F/O I. Smith when, as he was coming into land behind his colleague, his wings began to drop, apparently stalling, and the Typhoon hit the end of the runway. It then went up on its nose and over on to its back. There was a very strong wind and it appeared that Clarke had hit Smith's slipstream. He was immediately taken to hospital, seriously injured. Sadly, it was discovered he had broken his neck and was paralysed from the waist down. A week later, eight Typhoons took off for a dive-bombing strike led by the CO. While heading for Beachy Head at deck level, the Typhoons were forced to climb through 4,000 feet of cloud ahead of them. All went through but one pilot, P/O P.J. Elfner, was reported missing. The op was cancelled; the remaining Typhoons returned to base an hour later. It was later learned Elfner had crashed into the sea off Beachy Head. April was not a very intensive month regarding ops, with just 60 sorties being flown. The stay at Funtington ended on 18 April and 439 returned to Hurn. The squadron flew over 130 sorties during May, a good result considering it had been sent to Hutton Cranswick for the period 11–20 May for an armament practice camp. On the debit side, a Typhoon was lost during the month; returning from a dive-bombing raid on marshalling yards near Douai, the CO's aircraft caught fire and crashed into a field near Ford. Fortunately, Norsworthy was unhurt. Operations continued in June, with rumours of the invasion of Occupied Europe rife. Just before the historic day, 439 lost one of its own while attacking a radar station at Saint Peter Port on the island of Guernsey. The target was attacked with bombs, but the leader, F/L J.W. Saville, a flight commander, was shot down by flak. His position was immediately taken over by F/L K.J. Fiset. The next day, the 6th, 439 provided support to the invasion forces by flying three ops, close to 30 sorties, during the day. No loss was recorded. Ground support continued for the next few days, 439 being airborne almost every day, only being grounded by bad weather on the 9th and 13th. While the squadron had only recorded aircraft damaged by flak since the invasion, and each time the aircraft was able to return to base, a Typhoon was lost on the 15th near Caen, on the third and last op of the day, during an attack on a bridge over the Orne (which had already been attacked on the two previous outings). The pilot, F/O J.W. Ross, evacuated his Typhoon and was seen floating down near Caen aerodrome; he was eventually captured and ended the war as a PoW. Operational activity intensified in the second half of June as the Allies sought to break out. On the 20th, 439 carried out four operations, the first time it had done so since becoming operational. Three days later, F/O J.A. Brown fell victim to an engine failure while returning from an armed recce. He baled out south of the Isle of Wight and was soon rescued. The squadron moved to France on the 27th, going to B.9/Lantheuil, but, as the runway was unserviceable, the Typhoons were diverted to No. 121 Wing's airfield. The trip ended badly for F/O B.P. Swingler whose engine failed and he was obliged to make a forced landing near B.5; the crash proved fatal for the Typhoon, which caught fire, but Swingler escaped unhurt. He had, however, been carrying personal and service clothing and equipment which served as additional fuel for the fire. The first sorties from the Continent were flown from 121 Wing's airstrip and, by the 30th, 439 had carried out 370 sorties. Now operating from its assigned airfield, 439 flew another 270 sorties in July. It was not without cost, however, as two pilots were lost. On 8 July, F/O F.M. Thomas was hit by flak crossing into enemy territory. He decided to return to Allied lines and chose to make an emergency landing at B.4 where No. 126 Wing was based. He overshot his first attempt to land and, on the second approach, his engine cut and the Typhoon spun into the ground. Still carrying bombs, one exploded on impact and the aircraft burst into flames, killing Thomas instantly. Ten days later, F/O J. Kalen was killed, shot down by flak while attacking the target. His Typhoon was seen to explode before hitting the ground.

August was tough. With the end of the Battle of Normandy in sight and German forces retreating, air support was in high demand;

more than 450 sorties were flown that month. This support ultimately proved costly even though the month did not start too badly. Indeed, 439 only lost its first Typhoon on the 8th when F/O I.W. Smith's engine packed up enroute to the target. He managed to stretch a long glide from 10,000 feet to crash land in a field near Saint-Germain-d'Ectot; he was soon back with the squadron. Four days later, it was another story, 439 losing two pilots in a single op on the afternoon of the 12th. That day, three bridges over the Orne were attacked, 439 participating with 12 Typhoons carrying 500-lb bombs. On the first show, once they were airborne, 439 split into three flights of four, one flight per bridge. Nos. 438 and 440 Squadrons had already carried out similar attacks on the same targets without success. When the Typhoons arrived over the target area, intense and accurate flak was encountered. The aircraft flown by F/O E.J. Allen was hit in the right wing and main fuel tanks at about 500 feet and fell out of control. He was last seen swinging safely down to earth under a gleaming white parachute. At almost the same instant, at 500 feet between the target and the town of Athis, F/O R.O. Moen was also hit, but in the radiator. He pulled away from his flight and headed roughly north-west, losing height rapidly as he went. Flying Officer J. Brown followed him down and saw Moen jettison his hood at 1,000 feet before he crashed near Saint-Pierre-la-Vieille. The aircraft exploded on impact, leaving very little hope of survival for Moen. For Allen, while there was hope he had survived, he was later found dead. He had been killed by ground fire. No losses were recorded the following week but 439 was hit by misfortune once more on the 19th when, during the third and last show of the day, an armed recce over the Orbec–Le Sap–Vimoutiers–Fervaques area, F/L W.K. Scharff and P/O R.A. Porrit were both posted missing. While Scharff was seen to be shot down while attacking METs, and seen to crash east of Vimoutiers, nobody knew what had happened to Porrit. He was later found in the wreckage of his aircraft; it was presumed he had been shot down by flak somewhere over the target. No more losses were recorded before the end of the month and, on the 30th, 439 moved to B.24/St André.

The Germans retreated rapidly towards their own border at the end of the Battle of Normandy, so the stay at Saint-André was short; on 2 September, 439 moved to B.48/Glisy, and soon followed this with another move on the 7th to B.58/Melsbroek in Belgium. The stay at Melsbroek, two weeks, would be the longest of the month. Indeed, on the 25th, the squadron moved to the Netherlands, B.78/Eindhoven, which would be its station for the next six months. With all of these moves, the number of sorties was clearly impacted; about 360 were carried out in September. In the meantime, 439 saw a new CO promoted, F/L Fiset taking over on the 12th, S/L Norsworthy being tour expired. At first, losses were light and, until the move to Eindhoven, just two pilots had been lost during the month. Led by the wing leader, W/C Judd, who was flying with 439, on the 9th the tasking was to bomb a concentration of barges on a canal near Vlissingen. When at the bottom of his dive, F/O G.W. Hewson was hit by flak. His aircraft began to stream glycol and then black smoke. Hewson chose to bale out. His parachute opened correctly but it took him to captivity. The day before the move to Eindhoven, F/O R.W. Vokey was killed while attacking METs near Oosterhout. It seems that he failed to recover from his dive, possibly owing to human error (maybe target fixation) as no flak was experienced during the attack. The first days at Eindhoven were intense. On the 26th, 439 celebrated its first success over the Luftwaffe. On the last op of the day, a fighter patrol, the Canadians finally made contact with German aircraft. At 17.50, eight Typhoons set off to patrol the Nijmegen–Arnhem area but, as dusk fell, one section was repeatedly attacked by US P-47 Thunderbolts, fortunately without major consequences. In the rapidly approaching darkness, F/L A.E. Monson, with the help of searchlights and flares, was able to catch a glimpse of a Ju88. He fired

Typhoon JR500/5V-X, armed with 500-lb bombs, starting up for a sortie from B.9/Lantheuil during the summer of 1944. Note the aircraft sports asymmetric spinner markings, a feature of some 143 Wing aircraft. Still part of 439's inventory, JR500 was later lost in a flying accident during the following November. *(CT Collection)*

Typhoon MN553/5V-K, with the classic red Maple Leaf painted in a white circle ahead of the cockpit. As with JR500 on the previous page, the individual letter is repeated on the nose between the spinner and the exhausts, a common practice for 439 during the summer of 1944.

a long burst at it but lost it before he could observe any definite result. Meanwhile, W/O W.A. Gray saw an Fw190, got in a quick burst and claimed it as damaged. Finally, F/O J.H. Stitt encountered another Ju88 at 7,000 feet and sent it down in flames. That was 439's first confirmed victory. Warrant Officer Gray, sadly, did not have time to celebrate his claim as he was killed the next day while attacking a goods train. His Typhoon was hit in the radiator, causing vapour to stream out. It later burst into flames and went into a steep dive, exploding on impact near Goch, the pilot, well into his second operational tour, still inside. The following day, the 28th, F/O M. Joseph-Anatole Côté ran out of fuel returning from the last sortie of the day and eventually made a safe forced landing in Luxembourg. Strangely, October resembled September, less the air-to-air claims, as the Allied offensive paused. Just over 400 sorties were carried out, four aircraft lost and two pilots killed. The first two Typhoons were both lost to the old enemy, flak. Pilot Officer A.C. McBride survived the forced landing on the 2nd after attacking a rail line at Issum, but F/O R.A. Johns was less lucky three days later on the way to Speelberg near Hemmerich; his aircraft blew up when it crashed into a steeple in Speelberg. The two other losses were sustained during the last week of October. On the 22nd, F/O R.V. Smith was shot down near 's-Hertogenbosch but evaded capture after baling out. On the 28th, F/O M.P. Laycock was killed during his attack dive, crashing four miles west of Deventer in the Netherlands. With the weather degrading in November, the number of sorties dropped to 260, but losses remained stable. On the 3rd, F/O R.N. MacDonald was up to carry out an air test at the same time as F/O R.H. Laurence. Both decided to start a mock-dogfight over Eindhoven. MacDonald's aircraft was seen to flick on recovering from a tight turn and hit a house. He was killed instantly. The first operational loss of the month occurred three days later. Despite the weather not being favourable, four operations were flown. Flying Officer Brown failed to return from the morning show. It is believed he went too low over the target and was caught in the blast of his own bombs as he was pulling up. His Typhoon began to stream glycol as Brown took a heading to the south in an attempt to reach Allied lines. On reaching Deventer, however, flak started to come up and intensified to the point where Brown was lost track of. It was subsequently learned he had been captured. On 11 November, F/O J.G. Fraser was hit by flak while engaged in a strike on Terherne. In a familiar scenario, the cooling system was hit and Fraser had no choice but to make a forced landing eight miles south of Sneek. However, he managed to evade capture. A week later, 439 lost two pilots on the same morning hop, both being caught by flak on the way to the target. Flying Officer J.G. Martin's Typhoon received a direct hit north-east of Roermond and he was forced to bale out. Sadly, his parachute malfunctioned and only opened in the treetops: he did not survive his injuries. Flying Officer R.A. Hiltz was luckier. His Typhoon was hit and he was obliged to make a forced landing. He was back at the squadron soon after, but his luck finally left him two days later when, while attacking a railway target, he was again shot down by flak. One of his wings was blown off and he was seen to spin into the ground east of Rhede in Germany. One could expect December would be a simple duplication of November, but it proved to be the busiest month of 439's entire wartime existence. On the 3rd, with 143 Wing, the unit was kept busy between Dorsten and Haltern despite heavy cloud making things difficult. A rail sweep was conducted during which four trains were strafed near Münster. In one attack, F/L W.L. Saunders was pulling up when several bursts of flak around him were seen by his wingman, F/O J.D. Sweeney, an American from Michigan. They both climbed into scattered cloud above the target but, upon breaking clear, Saunders had disappeared. The same day, S/L Fiset, tour expired, was replaced by F/L R.G. Crosby, a flight commander, the latter assuming the role two days later. He had to manage the first loss under his command on the 15th when, during a weather recce by four Typhoons led by Crosby, F/L C.A. Lambert was killed. During the flight, the section of four discovered a train and dropped their bombs on it, following up with a strafing run and leaving the train heavily damaged. After climbing out, Crosby resumed an easterly course, crossing the railway north of Haltern, a bad idea as it turned out

A native of Vancouver, Gordon Crosby enlisted in September 1940 and, once his training was completed, was retained in Canada as an instructor. He was finally sent overseas in February 1943 and started a tour of operations the following July with a Typhoon unit, 56 Sqn, until 3 January 1944 when he was shot down over France. He managed to evade capture and arrived at Gibraltar in April. Repatriated to Canada, he was back in Britain in August and initially posted to 438 before moving to 439 in November in anticipation of assuming command two weeks later, S/L Fiset being tour expired. On 22 January 1945, however, he was posted missing again before being reported safe five days later. His war was over; he was eventually repatriated in May.

as they encountered a heavy barrage of flak. The Typhoon flown by Lambert received a direct hit and his engine cut. He attempted a belly landing and picked a large field. Sadly, he overshot slightly and his aircraft went through a clump of trees, tearing a wing off and turning over on its back. Lambert did not survive the crash. By the end of December, the Battle of the Bulge was raging and, when the weather was good enough to intervene, the Typhoons were sent to support the Americans fighting in the area. In the early hours of 24 December, 439 was airborne and headed for the Cologne area to seek out road transport. A few isolated vehicles were found and shot up, but they soon found themselves attacked by US P-47 Thunderbolts south-east of Duren. Flight Lieutenant Kenneth F. Sage turned into the attack and was badly hit but managed to return to base. The Typhoon was only good for scrap. Flight Sergeant W.A. Wright was less fortunate and was shot down in flames. He managed to bale out but his parachute streamed and he was killed. Sage returned to ops later that day only to be shot down and killed by flak near Mayern; he was seen to flick over and crash to his death. Two more Typhoons were wrecked two days later on return from an op, the first after an undercarriage malfunction, and the second after damage sustained by flak. Both pilots survived. The next day, F/O B.E. Bell fell victim to flak when he was hit near Saint-Vith during an armed recce. He became a PoW. Two days later, the 29th, 439 was present in the Coesfeld area for armed recces. A number of trains had just been shot up when F/O Laurence saw a Typhoon being shot at by an Fw190 (he did not yet know a section of Typhoons from No. 168 Squadron, at the time part of the wing, had just been engaged). He gave chase at once, but he and his wingman were then attacked by about ten Fw190s. Laurence fled, pursued for some way until just one long-nose Fw190 remained on his tail; he made a number of tight turns, during which the Fw190 suddenly flicked over and crashed, bursting into flames. Laurence was then attacked by another fighter, a Bf109 this time, but this too rolled over and crashed, blowing up, before Lawrence could fire a shot. This engagement was not one sided, however, as W/O S.A. Church was shot down and became a PoW.

On 1 January 1945, 75 German fighters swooped on Eindhoven. When the first warning came out, 439's pilots were sitting around in the crew room awaiting the return of the weather recce. In 20 minutes, the Germans strafed all they could; when they left, one of 439's Typhoons was burning and another had been damaged. The returning weather recce section was caught in the middle of this big mess. They met about 15 Fw190s heading for Eindhoven and the four Typhoons were immediately engaged. While F/O S. Angelini was shot down and killed, Flying Officers Laurence and Fraser each claimed two Fw190s, although one of Laurence's claims was later amended to a probable. On the other hand, he received an immediate DFC! Squadron activity was not disrupted much as an armed recce was carried out without incident in the afternoon. Actually, 2TAF was not massively affected by Operation *Bodenplatte*; just a couple of hours were needed to return to taskings as weather permitted. The weather did indeed reduce operational activity as, during January, just over 200 sorties were carried out. On the 14th, the B Flight CO, F/L Côté, was posted missing after he was hit by flak attacking a bridge east of Zwölle. He made a successful forced landing four miles from the target in German-held territory; he eventually managed to evade capture. Flying Officer J.D. Sweeney did not get this chance when he was shot down on the 20th as he became a PoW. Misfortune hit 439 heavily two days later during the last show of the day, a dive-bombing op near Uetterach . The CO, who was leading, was hit by flak and his aircraft disintegrated in mid-air after the bombs were released. Crosby's aircraft had blown up, but he was thrown clear, suffering a dislocated right shoulder. He managed to get his parachute open at 1,000 feet, landing in woodland where he lay wrapped in his parachute and in great pain while searching German troops passed close by. He was badly shaken the next day when the same area was bombed again. As he was only four miles from Allied lines, he made his way past sentries and patrols to reach safety. His war was over and his position was assumed by S/L J.H. Beatty. During this fateful mission, other Typhoons were also hit; the engine of the aircraft flown by F/O W. Kubicki gave enough trouble that he was obliged to make a forced landing near Eersel in the Netherlands, in the Allied lines. He was safe, but the aircraft was never repaired. In February, the weather improved but losses remained low. A Typhoon was wrecked during a test flight by W/O B. Propas on the 10th; engine failure was the cause. The Typhoon caught fire and Propas was dragged out but not before suffering burns to his face and a fracture to the base of his skull. The second and last loss of the month occurred on the 22nd when F/L Swingler was shot down and killed near Bocholt during a dive-bombing op. He had noticed a lone transport vehicle and, after making one orbit, he dove on it, followed by the squadron. Flak immediately opened up. They had stumbled into a flak trap; it was too late for Swingler who never had a chance. He had just arrived the day before to take over A Flight. February, however, was marked by another event. On the 14th, German Me262 jet fighter-bombers were sent out to attack Nijmegen, Kleve and Gennep. On their

'Jim' Beatty, from Saskatchewan, enlisted in the RCAF in June 1941. He was trained in Canada and was posted, in April 1942, as an NCO to 132 Sqn to fly Kittyhawks. He received his commission in August the same year. In October 1943, he joined 111 Sqn, again on Kittyhawks, as it had been selected for overseas service in the UK as part of 2TAF. On arrival in the UK in early 1944, the unit was re-designated No. 440 (RCAF) Squadron and converted to the Hawker Typhoon. He participated in the invasion of Europe and became a flight commander in August. In October, Beatty was sent to the UK for a rest. In January 1945, he returned to operations as OC 439 Sqn, again on Typhoons of course, and led the unit until its disbandment in August 1945. In the meantime, in June, he had been awarded the DFC. Repatriated to Canada in September, he left the RCAF the following month.

return leg, they were intercepted by a quartet of 439 Typhoons which were re-forming after having strafed a train. The Canadians, at 7,000 feet, spotted two Me262s flying at 3,000 feet; both formations were headed in the same direction. The Me262 was, of course, a speedy aircraft and Allied fighters could generally only catch them with the advantage of height. The Typhoons had their chance to intercept the two Me262s. They immediately dived to attack and F/L C.L. Shaver was the first to get in a good position, line astern and slightly below, to open fire with a two-second burst at 100 yards, but nothing happened. Shaver continued to close and raised his sight a bit. At 50 yards, he fired again. This time the Me262 exploded, forcing Shaver to fly through the debris. On his side, F/O H. Fraser sealed the fate of the second Me262 with a burst of three seconds from 400 yards, closing to 50 yards just as the Me262 disappeared into cloud. He saw the left engine fall off the Me262 before the jet hit the ground and burst into flames. March proved more deadly, with three pilots killed in action and a fourth Typhoon wrecked, while over 500 sorties were flown. The first to lose his life was one of the victorious pilots who had shot down an Me262 on 14 February; F/L Shaver was killed by flak on 2 March near Dülmen. He was followed by F/O W. Anderson on the 24th, also shot down by flak near Dingden, and F/L W.G. Davies on the 30th, another victim of the flak near Lengerich. The lucky guy was F/O A.W. Saunders who had a tyre blow on landing while returning from ops; he survived the subsequent crash. At the end of the month, after more than six months based there, 439 left Eindhoven on the 29th and moved to Germany and B.100/Goth. The stay was short, however, as, on 2 April, the squadron was sent to Warmwell to attend an armament practice camp which was completed on the 21st. One accident was recorded at Warmwell when the undercarriage of the Typhoon flown by Murray Hallford collapsed on landing. The next day, 439 was sent back to the Continent and took up residence at B.150/Hustedt in Germany. That would be the unit's final base of

F/L Clarence Shaver shows a piece of his Me262 to S/L Beatty and F/O A.H. Fraser after their encounter with the jets on 14 February.

Pilots of 439 Sqn at Eindhoven in March 1945.
Back: Warrant Officers E.F. Kidd and R.J. Roach, Flying Officers F.M. Hallford, D.G. Cleghorn and A.H. Fraser, F/L W.G. Davis (†30.03.45), Flying Officers A.W. Saunders and W. Kubicki, Flight Lieutenants M.J. Whelan and V.H.J. Le Gear, and Flying Officers S.D. Marlatt, J.L. Harrison and J.H. Cook.
Front: Flying Officers H.R. Herod, A.E. Derouin, W. Anderson (†24.03.45) and A.C. McBride, S/L W.L. Beatty (CO), Flight Lieutenants J.O. Gray (USA), M. Harrison (Adj) and A.W .Breck, and F/O J. Roberts.

the war. Operations resumed on the 23rd with two armed recces in the afternoon. While the first show was uneventful, the second was not with F/L J. D. McCullough shot down by flak while attacking METs near Ratzeburg. He managed to make a forced landing nearby and was taken prisoner soon after. The squadron flew every single day for the rest of April and, in all, flew 180 operational sorties, followed by 105 more in the first four days of May. On 2 May, F/L S.D. Marlatt led the squadron on a search for convoys in the area east of Lübeck. Anti-personnel bombs were carried by the seven-aircraft formation. The weather was poor over base and they could not get over 1,500 feet until after they crossed the Elbe. The ceiling lifted to 7,000 feet east of Ratzenburger Lake and visibility was very good. The Canadians spotted some targets to attack. As one section was attacking, the other section was orbiting as cover. Shortly before midday, the orbiting section suddenly saw a Fieseler Storch flying west at about 50 feet. It was immediately chased; the German pilot saw the attack coming and tried to land in a field but before he could do so, F/L J.O. Gray, a Texan, fired a long burst and the Fieseler exploded and burned. Then another small aircraft (later claimed as an Fw44) was seen at approximately the same position, also flying at zero feet. Flight Lieutenant J.H. Cook gave it a short burst and it hit the ground, breaking into several pieces. By this time, the Canadians were running short of petrol and all assumed course to base. The good day was followed by a bad one. In the first show of the morning, F/O G.F. Burden was shot down and killed by flak while attacking a train near Pinneberg. He was the squadron's last operational loss of the war.
On 29 May, 439 moved to B.166/Flensberg where it stayed until disbandment on 26 August. The number of flights was reduced during this period of time and only consisted of practice flying. Some incidents were recorded but fortunately without loss of life. On 22 June, W/O R.J. Roach made a wheels-up landing at B.160, the aircraft was not repaired and, on 29 July, MN631 caught fire on engine start at base and here too the aircraft was not repaired .

Typhoon RB402/5V-P at Eindhoven in March 1945.

Claims - 439 Squadron (Confirmed and Probable)

Date	Pilot	SN	Origin	Type	Serial	Code	Nb	Cat.
26.09.44	F/O Johnny H. **Stitt**	Can./ J.17529	RCAF	Ju88	**MN379**	5V-E	1.0	C
29.12.44	F/O Robert H. **Laurence**	Can./ J.20602	RCAF	Fw190D	**RB233**	5V-F	1.0	C
				Bf109			1.0	C
01.01.45	F/O Robert H. **Laurence**	Can./ J.20602	RCAF	Fw190	**RB233**	5V-F	1.0	C
							1.0	P
	F/O Alexander H. **Fraser**	Can./ J.37029	RCAF	Fw190	**RB281**	5V-X	1.0	C
				Fw190D			1.0	C
14.02.45	F/L Lyal C. **Shaver**	Can./ J.17058	RCAF	Me262	**MN144**		1.0	C
	F/O Alexander H. **Fraser**	Can./ J.37029	RCAF	Me262	**RB281**	5V-X	1.0	C
02.05.45	F/L James O. **Gray**	Can./ J16545	(US)/RCAF	Fi156	**SW524**	5V-F	1.0	C
	F/L Jack H. **Cook**	Can./ J.9454	RCAF	Fw44	**RB477**		1.0	C

Total: 11.0

Summary of the aircraft lost on Operations - 439 Squadron

Date	Pilot	S/N	Origin	Serial	Code	Fate
10.04.44	P/O Paul J. **Elfner**	Can./ J.22281	RCAF	**JR264**	5V-H	†
24.05.44	S/L Hugh H. **Norsworthy**	Can./ J.5114	RCAF	**MN516**	5V-W	-
05.06.44	F/L John W. **Saville**	Can./ J.8146	RCAF	**MN210**	5V-U	†
15.06.44	F/O John W. **Ross**	Can./ J.22382	RCAF	**MN417**		**PoW**
23.06.44	F/O Raymond A. **Brown**	Can./ J.21136	RCAF	**MN663**		-
27.06.44	F/O Bernard P. **Swingler**	Can./ J.21837	RCAF	**MN776**		-
08.07.44	F/O Frank McD. **Thomas**	Can./ J.20648	RCAF	**MN464**	5V-N	†
18.07.44	F/O John **Kalen**	Can./ J.21856	RCAF	**MN574**		†
08.08.44	F/O Ivan W. **Smith**	Can./ J.22244	RCAF	**JR521**	5V-M	-
12.08.44	F/O Ralph O. **Moen**	Can./ J.22034	RCAF	**MN310**	5V-U	†
	F/O Ernest J. **Allen**	Can./ J.20587	RCAF	**MN553**	5V-K	†
19.08.44	P/O Robert A. **Porrit**	Can./ J.21202	RCAF	**MN401**	5V-G	†
	F/L William K. **Scharff**	Can./ J.7814	RCAF	**PD448**		†
09.09.44	F/O Gaele W. **Hewson**	Can./ J.21152	RCAF	**MP152**		**PoW**
24.09.44	F/O Richard W. **Vokey**	Can./ J.25397	RCAF	**PD465**	5V-Y	†
27.09.44	W/O2 William A. **Gray**	Can./ R.129277	RCAF	**PD458**		†
28.09.44	F/O M.J. Anatole **Côté**	Can./ J.14529	RCAF	**MN375**	5V-S	-
02.10.44	P/O Alaistair C. **McBride**	Can./ J.85728	RCAF	**MN379**	5V-E	-
05.10.44	F/O Royce A. **Johns**	Can./ J.21959	RCAF	**MN765**		†
22.10.44	F/O Roy V. **Smith**	Can./ J.27992	RCAF	**MP136**		**Eva.**
28.10.44	F/O Maurice P. **Laycock**	Can./ J.22035	RCAF	**MN870**	5V-P	†
06.11.44	F/O James A. **Brown**	Can./ J.28760	RCAF	**MN345**	5V-G	**PoW**
11.11.44	F/O John G. **Fraser**	Can./ J.36722	RCAF	**MN547**		**Eva.**
19.11.44	F/O Robert A. **Hiltz**	Can./ J.37855	RCAF	**MN537**		-
	F/O John G. **Martin**	Can./ J.37648	RCAF	**PD607**		†
21.11.44	F/O Robert A. **Hiltz**	Can./ J.37855	RCAF	**MN124**		†
03.12.44	F/L William L. **Saunders**	Can./ J.22803	RCAF	**MN348**		†
15.12.44	F/L Charles A. **Lambert**	Can./ J.7827	RCAF	**PD478**		†
24.12.44	F/L Kenneth F. **Sage**	Can./ C.1191	RCAF	**JR506**	5V-X	-
	F/Sgt William A.**Wright**	Can./ R.74061	RCAF	**PD492**		†
	F/L Kenneth F. **Sage**	Can./ C.1191	RCAF	**MN894**		†
26.12.44	F/O Walter **Kubicki**	Can./ J.25140	RCAF	**MN482**	5V-S	-
	F/O John D. **Sweeney**	Can./ J.35843	(US)/RCAF	**PD459**		-
27.12.44	F/O Bernard E. **Bell**	Can./ J.44311	RCAF	**MP145**		**PoW**
29.12.44	W/O1 Stanley A. **Church**	Can./ R.87186	RCAF	**MN791**		**PoW**
01.01.45	F/O Samuel **Angelini**	Can./ J.37114	RCAF	**MN589**		†
	destroyed in air raid	-	-	**MN869**	5V-A	-
	destroyed in air raid	-	-	**RB257**	5V-S	-
14.01.45	F/L M.J. Anatole **Côté**	Can./ J.14529	RCAF	**RB204**		**Eva.**
20.01.45	F/O John D. **Sweeney**	Can./ J.35843	(US)/RCAF	**RB317**		**PoW**
22.01.45	F/O Walter **Kubicki**	Can./ J.25140	RCAF	**MN424**	5V-Y	-
	S/L Robert G. **Crosby**	Can./ C.22655	RCAF	**MP134**	5V-Z	**Eva.**
22.02.45	F/L Bernard P. **Swingler**	Can./ J.21837	RCAF	**MP151**	5V-R	†
02.03.45	F/L Clarence L. **Shaver**	Can./ J.17058	RCAF	**MN144**	5V-H	†
22.03.45	F/O Adam W. **Saunders**	Can./ J.37015	RCAF	**PD451**	5V-A	-
24.03.45	F/O William **Anderson**	Can./ J.36997	RCAF	**MN936**	5V-Q	†
30.03.45	F/L William G. **Davis**	Can./ J.29881	RCAF	**RB435**		†
02.04.45	F/O Donald G. **Cleghorn**	Can./ J.23864	RCAF	**MN581**		**PoW**

23.04.45	F/L John D. **McCullough**	Can./ J.16210	RCAF	**SW525**		**PoW**
03.05.45	F/O George F. **Burden**	Can./ J.88715	RCAF	**SW443**	5V-M	†

Total: 50

Anatole Coté from Quebec City was posted to 439 in September 1944 and pancaked his Typhoon twice. The first time was on 28 September, when he ran out of fuel, and the second time was on 14 January 1945, after being hit by flak. Both times, he survived, but the second forced landing was inside the enemy lines; he managed to evade capture and was hidden for 80 days by the Dutch until the region was liberated. Note the spinner, markings sometimes used by 143 Wing Typhoons.

Summary of the aircraft lost by accident - 439 Squadron

Date	*Pilot*	*S/N*	*Origin*	*Serial*	*Code*	*Fate*
17.02.44	*Set on fire by heater*	-	-	**MN213**		-
20.02.44	F/O Elton L. **Dixon**	Can./ J.29073	RCAF	**R8971**		†
04.04.44	P/O Andrew C. **Clarke**	Can./ J.22000	RCAF	**JR324**	5V-M	**Inj.**
03.11.44	F/O Ralph N. **MacDonald**	Can./ J.21003	RCAF	**JR500**	5V-X	†
10.02.45	W/O2 Bernard **Propas**	Can./ R.164360	RCAF	**MN480**		**Inj.**
17.04.45	F/O Frederick M. **Halford**	Can./ J.38923	RCAF	**RB387**		-
22.06.45	W/O2 Richard J. **Roach**	Can./ R.80946	RCAF	**MP117**		-
29.07.45	*Engine fire on start-up*	-	-	**MN691**	5V-R	-

Total: 8

February 1944
August 1945

Victories - confirmed or probable claims: 1.0

First operational sortie: 30.03.44
Last operational sortie: 21.04.45

Number of sorties: *ca.* **4,200**

Total aircraft written-off: 60

Aircraft lost on operations: 55
Aircraft lost in accidents: 5

Squadron code letters:
I8

Commanding Officers

S/L William H. Pentland(†)	Can./ J.3204	RCAF	08.02.44	07.10.44
S/L Alonzo E. Monson	Can./ J.22010	(US)/RCAF	08.10.44	15.12.44
S/L Harold O. Gooding	Can./ J.10608	RCAF	15.12.44	10.03.45
S/L Robert E. Coffey (†)	Can./ J.10256	(US)/RCAF	10.03.45	30.07.45
S/L Alonzo E. Monson	Can./ J.22010	(US)/RCAF	04.08.45	26.08.45

Squadron Usage

Previously known as No. 111 Squadron RCAF, 440 was one of the very few units of the RCAF on the Home Front to engage the Japanese in the Aleutians, and to make claims against them. Highly experienced, it was logical to select 111 to join the RCAF Overseas. Upon its arrival in Europe, the unit was renamed No. 440 (RCAF) Squadron on 8 February 1944. The changeover took place at Ayr in Scotland. The squadron was at the time under the command of S/L W.H. Pentland and was integrated into No. 143 Wing. Earmarked to fly the Hawker Typhoon alongside the other squadrons of the wing, 440 received Hawker Hurricanes to help with the transition. At the end of February, five Typhoons were on charge alongside 11 Hurricanes. Practice continued in March with a move to Hurn on the 18th. Five Typhoons, led by the experienced F/O R. Milne, left at 10.00 for the new base but the forma-

''Bill' Pentland was from Alberta and enlisted in the RCAF in May 1940. Upon completion of his training, Pentland was posted overseas and joined 1 Sqn RCAF in England. In February 1941, he moved to 2 Sqn RCAF, also in England, which was renamed No. 402 (RCAF) Squadron in March. On 18 September, he opened his score by claiming a Bf109 damaged. In February 1942, he was posted to the recently formed No. 417 (RCAF) Squadron which deployed to the Middle East in April. He completed his tour in June 1943, by which time he had become a flight commander, and had made all his claims of the war: one shared confirmed and two damaged (one shared). He then returned to Canada for a rest. In December 1943, Pentland returned to operational duties, joining 111 Sqn as it embarked for the UK. On 8 February 1944, this unit became No. 440 (RCAF) Squadron and Pentland assumed command the same day. He led the unit until 7 October when he was killed in action, near Wesel in Germany. He had been awarded a DFC in September.

Pilots of 440 at B.9 in August 1944.
Front: Flying Officers C.F. Osborne (Adj) and R.G. Hattie, Flight Lieutenants R. Dunne (MO) and C.W. Hicks (†08.08.44), Flying Officers A. Frombolo (USA, PoW 28.11.44) and W.E. Ward, S/L D.A .Brownlee (Airfield Adm Officer), Flying Officers R.E. Collis (Eng) and B. Daykin (IO), and WO2 R.A. Watson.
Standing: Flying Officers J.A.D Gordon and F.J. Crowley (†11.11.44), W/C M.T. Judd (RAF, 143 Wing Leader), G/C P.Y. Davoud (OC 143 Wing), S/L W.H. Pentland (OC 440 Sqn, †07.10.44), Flight Lieutenants H.O. Gooding (later CO in December) and J. Bonner (Airfield Adj), and Flying Officers D.C. Campbell and R.H. Milne (PoW 19.08.44).
Sitting on the wings: Flying Officers J.H. Beatty (later CO 439 Sqn in January 1945), D.V. Wright, D.F. English, R.J.C. Gardner and G.D. Russell, F/Sgt N.L .Gordon, and Flying Officers J.A. Stewart (RAF) and R.E.G. McCurdy (†13.08.44).
Standing on the wing: F/L R.W. Doidge (†20.10.44) and F/O J.F. Dewar (†12.08.44).
On the spinner: F/O J.S. Colville (†18.09.44) with F/L D.E. Jenvey (†25.03.45) and F/O JAP Simard behind him.

tion was separated in cloud and P/O K.O. Mitchell was posted missing. It was later discovered he had hit high ground while still in cloud. He was the squadron's first casualty. By the end of March, 440 was ready and a first op was planned for the 28th. Ten Typhoons led by the wing leader, W/C Davidson, took off at 14.50 for a sweep but because of the bad weather, a U-turn was ordered and the formation landed at 15.20. False start aside, the squadron kicked off two days later with a search for shipping in the Channel Islands with the same number of Typhoons, once more led by W/C Davidson. While it and another sweep over Cherbourg and Caen the next day proved uneventful, 440 was on its way.
The squadron moved to Funtington on 3 April. Bad weather over the following days prevented much operational flying, with just one op on the 8th and another on the 12th. More sweeps followed during the month to bring the number of sorties for April to 110; nothing major was reported. In May, sorties doubled but not without loss. On 4 May, F/O W.D. Peacock was killed on the return leg from a Ramrod over the Continent. His Typhoon struck the mooring cable of a captive balloon and fell to the ground out of control near Eastleigh; Peacock was killed on impact. On 22 May, 440 lost its first Typhoon to enemy action when, while attacking a Direction Finding Station at Arromanches, F/O A.A. Watkins was hit by flak. He was seen to bale out and land safely in the water five miles off the French coast. He was last seen floating in his dinghy but the air–sea rescue (ASR) Walrus and fighter escort were unable to locate him before darkness fell. A second rescue team was sent out the next day, but Watkins was not found; he would spend five-and-a-half days on the water before finally being spotted and picked up by a Walrus. The squadron lost another Typhoon the day after Watkins was shot down when F/O F.J. Crowley was hit by flak off Cherbourg and baled out after the aircraft caught fire. He was rescued soon after by a Walrus. Aside from these operational losses, F/O N. Stusiak was killed in a flying accident on the 27th while practicing aerobatics, making May a rather sad month for the squadron. Then, two dozen uneventful sorties were flown in the lead up to D-Day. That day, 440 carried out close to 30 sorties. All went well until the evening when the Typhoons were

The Normandy airfields were right in the middle of the season's crops as can been seen here with I8-E (beleived to be MN397) in August 1944.

sent south of Caen for an armed recce in the search for MTs and tanks. Flying Officer L.R. Allman did not return. While strafing vehicles, he was apparently hit by flak near Manvieux. Flak was accurate as two other Typhoons were hit and both crashed on landing; neither pilots nor airframes were lost. The next day, three ops were flown in support of the landing troops. The squadron paid a high price as flak shot down three Typhoons and seriously damaged two others. The three missing Typhoons were lost on the same strike which was carried out between 0730 and 0855 despite bad weather and a ceiling at 1,500 feet. It was the first show of the day, an armed recce in the Caen–Falaise area looking for German vehicles. Some were found south of Caen but the flak proved heavy and accurate. Flying Officers W.J. Mahagan and S.V. Garside were both killed while F/O R.W. Doidge managed to evacuate his Typhoon, after it was hit in the radiator, and evade capture, returning to the squadron on the 10th. The squadron retrieved one pilot only to lose another two days later when F/L J.G. Gohl was forced to bale out after experiencing engine trouble, probably caused by flak, following an attack on the village of Varaville. Sadly, his parachute was seen to catch on the tailplane of his aircraft and Gohl went down with the Typhoon. The next few days involved intensive flying and while several Typhoons were hit by flak or experienced engine failure, obliging a landing on an emergency landing strip, no losses were recorded until the 23rd. While strafing vehicles near Juvigny, F/O R.G. Hattie was shot down in flames. He managed to bale out safely and landed just inside Allied lines. No more losses followed before the end of the month during which 370 sorties were achieved. The last sorties of June were flown from B.9/Lantheuil in France, 440 arriving there on the 28th. While July saw only 230 sorties carried out, the month continued to be costly with no less than seven Typhoons lost. Nevertheless, the first fortnight was free of any loss, but the bad run started on the 16th. A dramatic accident occurred that day on take-off for another op. The Typhoon flown by W/O C.J. McConvey veered off the runway, dipping its right wing into the ground, possibly after having struck an aircraft of 438 Squadron parked in a bay. The right bomb exploded and killed the pilot and two groundcrew, Leading Aircraftmen Wilman and Holmes, of No. 6438 Echelon who were working nearby. The next day, Hattie was shot down a second time when he was hit by flak while attacking German gun positions. Once again, he managed to bale out and landed between the lines. He was eventually picked up by an armoured recce car of the 15th Scottish Division but was wounded this time. Warrant Officer Richard A. Watson was also shot down by flak the day after, the 18th. He was blown out of his aircraft, breaking through the harness and canopy. The first thing he remembered was coming to mid-air and looking for the ripcord. He landed safely and unhurt behind German lines, suffering just a severe headache from the shake-up. While coming down in his parachute, the Germans had been machine gunning him; his parachute was hit several times. One

Typhoon MN413/I8-T being removed from the strip at B.9 after a wheels-up landing on 1 August 1944. The pilot, F/Sgt N.L. Gordon, escaped unhurt.
(CT Collection)

Typhoon MP149/I8-P *Pulverizer II* taxiing out from its dispersal at B.78 Eindhoven amid fuel and other stores in October 1944. *(CT Collection)*

20mm shell ripped through his Mae West on the way down. After landing, he threw off the Mae West and dinghy and ran for shelter as an artillery shell exploded a few yards from where he had thrown his gear. Shells and bombs continued to explode close by so Watson dug a slit trench with his hands and remained in it until the British Army advanced. The squadron experienced another fateful day, on the 26th, with three Typhoons wrecked. The CO, S/L Pentland, while taking off for the first show of the day, experienced an engine failure on the way to the target and had to make an emergency landing at Carpiquet in France, which proved fatal for the Typhoon, but he emerged unscathed despite one of his bombs exploding during the crash and blowing off the tail. The two other Typhoons were lost on the second and last show of the day late in the afternoon. Attacking troops forming up, F/L D.C.W. Stults and F/Sgt F.S. Gordon were both shot down by flak. Both baled out successfully over the Allied lines, but Stults suffered burns to varying degrees.

In August, 440, along with 143 Wing, was heavily engaged in support of the advancing Allied forces, with the peak being the Battle of Falaise. About 450 sorties were carried during the month and four Typhoons were lost to enemy action. The first casualty occurred on the 8th during a dive-bombing attack on a German HQ in a big manor near Ussy. Four direct hits were scored with the balance of the bombs bursting in the target area. Flak was present and active, of course, and F/L C.W. Hicks received a direct hit while pulling out of the dive. His aircraft was seen to burst into flames and crash close to the target. Four days later, F/O J.F. Dewar was shot down and killed by flak while in his dive to bomb a bridge at Pont-d'Ouilly. The next day, Dewar was followed in the list of killed in action by F/O R.E.G. McCurdy, who was shot down by flak attacking METs near Flers, and F/O J.S. Colville, who met the same fate near Vimoutiers on the 18th while also attacking METs. The next day, Ramsay Milne was posted missing from the third operation of the day near Le Sap; he managed to get out of his Typhoon and landed successfully, but behind enemy lines. He was captured and became a PoW. He was the last loss for August. The Battle of Falaise now over, German forces began a long but fast retreat. Various moves were therefore made to try to follow the rapidly advancing Allied troops. On 31 August, 440 moved to B.24/Saint-André, then to B.48/Glisy on 3 September, and B.58/Melsbroek in Belgium on the 6th which would become 440's home for the following two weeks. Despite these moves, the squadron managed to maintain a high rate of operations with close to 400 sorties flown. It was a great achievement considering no ops were flown in the first week of September. However, during the ferry flights between airfields, one Typhoon was lost at Illiers l'Évêque (B.26) when MN764 overshot on landing and hit an obstruction. The pilot, F/O J. Campbell, was injured. On the operational side, the loss rate dropped considerably with only two losses, only one

Bill Pentland was replaced by an American pilot serving with the RCAF, 'Cody' Monson, posted in from 439. Hailing from California, he was a mechanic when he decided to enlist in the RCAF in November 1941. Initially retained as a flying instructor, he was eventually posted to an operational squadron, 125 RCAF, in September 1943 and was sent with it to Europe where the unit was renamed No. 439 (RCAF) Squadron. He became tour expired in December and was repatriated with a DFC. Monson was replaced by 'Hal' Gooding who had more experience, having served with 111 Sqn RCAF since March 1942. He also eventually became tour expired in March 1945.

of them possibly caused by enemy action. On 9 September, F/Sgt N.L. Gordon experienced a glycol leak on return from an armed recce during which METs were strafed. He had possibly been hit by flak and ultimately made a crash landing near Brussels, sealing the fate of his Typhoon. The next day, Francis Crowley's engine failed on take-off for another armed recce and he was forced to make a dead-stick landing just before reaching the runway. The aircraft turned over, bounced and caught fire; somehow, Crowley managed to extricate himself from the wreckage. On the 26th, a move was made to B.78/Eindhoven in the Netherlands and, like its sister units, 440 would stay there until the end of March, the front having now stabilised.
However, the number of sorties and losses remained stable in October, but with one major difference, the loss of the CO on the 7th. The third and final show of that day was a dive-bombing attack on railway targets near Hamminkeln. The Typhoon was seen to explode just as Pentland dropped his bombs, surely hit by flak. He only had to fly three more trips to complete his second tour. The previous day, F/L C.S. Aistrop had been shot down by flak and killed while attacking the marshalling yards at Geldern, making two losses in two days. Pentland was replaced by newly promoted S/L A. Monson, an American serving in the RCAF, posted in from 439 Squadron. After two weeks free of loss, another Typhoon went down to flak on the 20th; while attacking rail lines near Nijverdal in the Netherlands, F/O R. Doidge, having evaded capture several months before, was hit by flak and spun in, leaving no hope of survival. A week later, 440 almost lost another CO when Monson was hit in the radiator by flak during an attack on a bridge in the Netherlands. He tried to no avail to nurse his Typhoon back and was obliged to abandon the aircraft close to the airstrip as the engine's temperature was rising too fast. He landed in the Allied lines and was back at the squadron within an hour. With the autumn weather coming in and worsening, 440 managed to carry out some 250 sorties in November. Despite this rather low figure, the loss ratio was high. On 11 November, F/O Crowley, one of the original pilots of the squadron, was shot down by flak and killed while attacking railway targets south-east of Staphorst in the Netherlands; after releasing his bombs, the Typhoon exploded before it pulled out of the dive. A week later, flak claimed yet another victim, F/O R.J. Reilly, who was last heard asking on the R/T to be directed to Allied lines as he was in trouble after an attack on a bridge north of Wassenburg in Germany. He never made it home as he crashed near the German/Dutch border. The next day, the 19th, F/O J.M. Cordick was killed by flak while attacking railway targets between Kempen and Geldern, his Typhoon exploding. He was followed by the loss of F/O J.L. Duncan, an American from Detroit, two days later on the 21st; he became a PoW after being hit by flak while attacking a train north-east of Horst in the Netherlands. On the 28th, F/O Anthony Frombolo, an American from Oakland, California, serving in the RCAF, met the same fate as he was hit by flak before reaching the target. He baled out and landed in the German lines. Support for the 21st Army continued in December, the number of sorties remaining stable, as did the losses; 440 was paying the highest price for victory among the wing's units. The month started badly with the loss of P/O A.W.E. Sugden who, exceptionally, was not shot down by flak. Having taken off on the 3rd for a support sortie, he was forced to return early owing to engine trouble. He had to land in a hurry and came in downwind. There was a brisk wind blowing and he ran off the end of the runway into the canal and was pinned in his Typhoon and drowned (his aircraft was later salvaged and repaired). Surprisingly, no other loss was recorded until the day before Christmas, giving hope the festive season would pass with no sorrow; the only other major event was the change of commander, Monson, at last tour expired, relinquishing command to S/L H.O. Gooding on the 15th. But the cruel reality of the war came back on the 24th when three pilots

P/O R.A. Watson climbing into his Typhoon with the assistance of two groundcrew at the end of November 1944. Watson was later involved in the furious dogfight on 1 January 1945 against JG 3, during which he claimed an Fw190 damaged. This claim was subsequently not allowed.

were killed in action. That day, four armed recces were carried out and F/O C.F.J. Harwood failed to return from the second, shot down by flak, south-east of Schleiden in Germany. The two other losses occurred on the next recce. Flying Officer D.H. Cumming and W.T. Dunkeld (from Pontiac, Michigan) were part of a formation acting as fighter cover for six Typhoons when they were caught by a lone Fw190 which shot them down in quick succession; both were killed. The next day, F/O H.J. Hardy was also hit by flak while strafing targets but he managed to make it close enough to base, in a heavily damaged Typhoon, to be able to abandon his aircraft. Happily, he was back at the squadron in time to enjoy Christmas dinner. Two days later, 440 celebrated another event: its first and only victory of the war. It happened on the only op of the day, in the Saint-Vith area during the Battle of the Bulge, with F/L Don Jenvey leading. After having released his bombs, Jenvey set course for home but discovered his section was not with him. He turned about and flew for about 30 seconds at 10,000 feet in the direction of the target. He sighted a Bf109 going straight up in front of him then turning steeply to the left. Jenvey climbed and turned, closing to 300 yards, firing a long burst and obtaining strikes on the left wing. The Bf109 spiralled down, doing a complete turn before he could close again. Jenvey closed from almost directly above and, within 50 yards, he fired again, observing hits all over both wings and cockpit, causing the wings to disintegrate. The hood and part of the cowling flew off. Jenvey saw the Bf109 diving to the ground but could not stay much longer in the area as he was immediately attacked by three other Bf109s. He tried to respond to the attack and discovered his guns had jammed, leaving no alternative but to break off and make for home. Don Jenvey enjoyed his victory for only a short time as he was shot down two days later on the 29th. Hit by flak, he managed, however, to make a forced landing in Germany behind enemy lines. He made his way to the Netherlands and was hidden by locals. Sadly, he was later betrayed and shot while escaping on 25 March 1945.
Eindhoven airfield was hit hard during Operation *Bodenplatte* on 1 January 1945. The squadron sustained 143 Wing's heaviest losses on the ground with nine Typhoons destroyed, including the wing leader's aircraft (W/C F.G. Grant) which was in 440's charge. Because of those losses, no operational flying was carried out for the next few days to allow time to recover; ops resumed on the 4th with a simple recce by four aircraft. Soon, 440 returned to its normal duties but the number of sorties was reduced to 180 in January, with three losses reported: F/O P.H. Kearse on the 21st, F/L H.N. Byers on the 23rd (both shot down and killed by flak), and P/O I.L. Gunnarson, who suffered an engine failure enroute for an armed recce on the 24th but managed to survive.
The level of activity was at least maintained throughout February and March and, with the weather getting better, the number of

Various scenes of Typhoons at Eindhoven, Winter 1944–1945. Above: RB389/I8-P Pulverizer IV replaced the previous I8-P, RB342 Pulverizer III, which was damaged and sent away on 24 February 1945.
Below: the undercarriage of F/O RM Gray's MN659/I8-E came down during a dive-bombing attack on 22 February 1945. Despite 'three greens', it collapsed on landing at Eindhoven. *(CT Collection - both)*

The last wartime 440 CO was another American, Bill Coffey from Illinois. He enlisted in the RCAF in June 1941 and at first served as a flying instructor until joining 118 Sqn in July 1943 to proceed overseas. He served with the subsequent 438 until being posted to 440 to command. Sadly, he was fatally injured in a vehicle accident on 1 August. He was awarded the DFC in January 1945 while flying with 438; a Bar followed in September after his death. He became one of the very few Americans to be awarded the DFC and Bar.

sorties increased: 375 in February and 475 in March. The last March sorties were flown from a new base, B.100/Goch in Germany, from the 30th, and a new CO, S/L R.E. Coffey, another American serving in the RCAF took over on the 10th following the departure of the tour-expired S/L Gooding. During that period, and especially in February, 440 remained 143 Wing's squadron with the highest loss rate, not necessarily in terms of Typhoons lost but pilots killed in action. In February, Flying Officers G.L. Passmore and W.R. Gibbs were lost to flak on the 2nd and the 28th respectively, while F/O J.F. Warrell was killed after he spun in while attacking trains north-west of Bocholt on the 3rd. Here flak seems not to have been responsible; it was more likely pilot error. However, flak was responsible for the loss of F/O J.D. Flintoft on the 24th but he managed to evade capture and was hidden by the Dutch. He eventually met up with British troops on 1 April, bringing in three German prisoners in the process, and was back with 440 two days later. In March, 440 recorded no deaths, the first time for months. That does not mean no Typhoons were wrecked though. On the 2nd, the aircraft flown by F/L W.J. McCarthy (from New York State) was damaged by flak while attacking railway targets and crashed at Eindhoven. The pilot was uninjured. On the 24th, F/O A.M. Scott crashed on take-off after having swung and the undercarriage collapsing under the stress. Repairs to the aircraft were never carried out and it was struck off charge the following October. The stay at Goch was short, another move taking place on the 10th when the squadron followed the wing to B.110/Osnabrück in Germany. With the German forces now collapsing, more moves followed. On the 19th, 440 went to B.150/Hustedt, its final wartime station. These moves did not prevent 440 from maintaining an intensive tempo of ops in support with over 450 sorties flown in April. Surprisingly, no casualties were recorded. April proved to be a 'short' month as, on the 21st, the squadron flew what was to be its last operation, a dive-bombing attack on the town of Achim in preparation for a direct assault by ground forces. As the army was late, the squadron was able to position for a really good attack and all bombs fell in the target area. The wing leader, W/C Grant, was leading the strike and was flying with 440; his aircraft was damaged during the dive. On return, the Typhoon was grounded but the repairs were never carried out and it was also eventually struck off charge in October. The next day, 440 flew to Warmwell to undertake an armament practice camp, which ended on 7 May. The squadron expected to return to B.150/Hustedt to continue combat operations but, by the time it arrived, Germany had surrendered. With peace in Europe, 2TAF reassigned its wings and squadrons. On 29 May, 440 moved to B.166/Flensburg where it would remain until it was disbanded on 26 August. This last chapter was not free of drama or accident, however. On 8 July, F/L H.T.C. Taylor, after a hydraulic system failure while returning from a short stay in Belgium and the Netherlands, was obliged to make a wheels-up landing at Nordholz, a US airfield, sealing the fate of the Typhoon. More devastating was the death of the CO on 30 July when he lost control of his jeep while driving from Flensburg to the airfield. He received a bad head injury and died two days later. Squadron Leader Monson returned to take command and remained in the role until the unit disbanded.

Claims - 440 Squadron (Confirmed and Probable)

Date	*Pilot*	*SN*	*Origin*	*Type*	*Serial*	*Code*	*Nb*	*Cat.*
27.12.44	F/L Donald E. **Jenvey**	Can./ J.11309	RCAF	Bf109	**MN641**	I8-B	1.0	C

Total: 1.0

Left: the only pilot who made a claim for a confirmed or probable kill, Don Jenvey of Ontario. He first enlisted in the RCN before being transferred to the RCAF. He instructed for many months before eventually joining an operational unit, 440, at the end of June 1944. He was shot down two days after he made his claim. He initially evaded capture but was killed on 25 March 1945 while trying to escape.

Right: John Flintoft from Quebec was shot down on 24 February but managed to evade capture for five weeks. Hidden by the Dutch, he finally met up with British troops on 1 April with three German prisoners!

Summary of the aircraft lost on Operations - 440 Squadron

Date	*Pilot*	*S/N*	*Origin*	*Serial*	*Code*	*Fate*
22.05.44	F/O Albert A. **Watkins**	Can./ J.26919	RCAF	**MN489**	I8-N	-
23.05.44	F/O Francis J. **Crowley**	Can./ J.26914	RCAF	**MN637**	I8-V	-
06.06.44	F/O Leonard R. **Allman**	Can./ J.13558	RCAF	**MN428**	I8-G	†
07.06.44	F/O Ronald W. **Doidge**	Can./ J.26406	RCAF	**MN257**	I8-D	**Eva.**
	F/O Wilfred J. **Mahagan**	Can./ J.11280	RCAF	**MN307**		†
	F/O Stanley V. **Garside**	Can./ J.5068	RCAF	**MN548**	I8-F	†
12.06.44	F/L James G. **Gohl**	Can./ J.8356	RCAF	**MN115**		†
23.06.44	F/O Robert G. **Hattie**	Can./ J.8356	RCAF	**MN171**	I8-E	-
16.07.44	W/O2 Carl J. **McConvey**	Can./ R.148645	RCAF	**MN770**	I8-L	†
17.07.44	F/O Robert G. **Hattie**	Can./ J.8356	RCAF	**MN715**		-
18.07.44	W/O2 Richard A. **Watson**	Can./ R.135831	RCAF	**MN644**	I8-T	-
26.07.44	F/L Douglas C. **Stults**	Can./ J.10565	RCAF	**MN369**		**Inj.**
	F/Sgt Nelson L. **Gordon**	Can./ R.176568	RCAF	**MN403**	I8-J	-
	S/L W illiam H. **Pentland**	Can./ J.3204	RCAF	**MN709**	I8-B	-
30.07.44	F/O John W. **Lippert**	Can./ J.27245	RCAF	**MN793**	I8-Z	†
08.08.44	F/L Clifford W. **Hicks**	Can./ J.26912	RCAF	**MN313**		†
12.08.44	F/O John F. **Dewar**	Can./ J.28180	RCAF	**MP122**	I8-T	†
13.08.44	F/O Roger E.G. **McCurdy**	Can./ J.21517	RCAF	**MN720**	I8-W	†
18.08.44	F/O John S. **Colville**	Can./ J.29167	RCAF	**MN929**	I8-Z	†
19.08.44	F/O Ramsay H. **Milne**	Can./ J.16142	RCAF	**MN154**	I8-R	**PoW**
09.09.44	F/Sgt Nelson L. **Gordon**	Can./ R.176568	RCAF	**MN817**	I8-S	-
10.09.44	F/O Francis J. **Crowley**	Can./ J.26914	RCAF	**MN796**		-
06.10.44	F/L Charles S. **Aistrop**	Can./ J.13484	RCAF	**MN805**	I8-Y	†
07.10.44	S/L William H. **Pentland**	Can./ J.3204	RCAF	**MN641**	I8-B	†
20.10.44	F/O Ronald W. **Doidge**	Can./ J.26406	RCAF	**PD469**	I8-E	†
29.10.44	S/L Alonzo E. **Monson**	Can./ J.22010	(us)/RCAF	**MN352**		-
11.11.44	F/O Francis J. **Crowley**	Can./ J.26914	RCAF	**MP124**	I8-A	†
18.11.44	F/O Robert J. **Reilly**	Can./ J.38349	RCAF	**MN475**	I8-A	†
19.11.44	F/O John M. **Cordick**	Can./ J.40775	RCAF	**MN801**	I8-F	†
21.11.44	F/O Jack L. **Duncan**	Can./ J.90433	(us)/RCAF	**PD523**	I8-Y	**PoW**
28.11.44	F/O Anthony **Frombolo**	Can./ J.28761	(us)/RCAF	**MP183**	I8-H	**PoW**

03.12.44	P/O Alfred E. **Sugden**	Can./ J.90713	RCAF	**MN251***	I8-F	†
24.12.44	F/O Charles F.J. **Harwood**	Can./ J.17954	RCAF	**MN453**	I8-J	†
	F/O Duncan H. **Cumming**	Can./ J.25086	RCAF	**MN665**	I8-X	†
	F/O William T. **Dunkeld**	Can./ J.25085	(us)/RCAF	**PD462**	I8-K	†
25.12.44	F/O Harry J. **Hardy**	Can./ J.20841	RCAF	**MP149**	I8-P	-
29.12.44	F/L Donald E. **Jenvey**	Can./ J.11309	RCAF	**RB201**	I8-L	**Eva./†**
01.01.45	*Damaged in air raid; not repaired*	-	-	**JR530**	I8-Y	-
	Destroyed in air raid	-	-	**MN569**		-
	Destroyed in air raid	-	-	**MN940**	I8-M	-
	Destroyed in air raid	-	-	**MN984**		-
	Destroyed in air raid	-	-	**MP139**	I8-W	-
	Destroyed in air raid	-	-	**PD595**	I8-X	-
	Destroyed in air raid	-	-	**PD621**		-
	Destroyed in air raid	-	-	**RB192**		-
	Destroyed in air raid	-	-	**RB205**	FGG	-
21.01.45	F/O Pearcy H. **Kearse**	Can./ J.25840	RCAF	**PD601**	I8-X	†
23.01.45	F/L Harold N. **Byers**	Can./ J.13485	RCAF	**RB325**	I8-X	†
24.01.45	P/O Ivar L.**Gunnarson**	Can./ J.88958	RCAF	**MN626**	I8-B	-
02.02.45	F/O Gerald L. **Passmore**	Can./ J.35987	RCAF	**PD493**	I8-F	†
03.02.45	F/O John F. **Warrell**	Can./ J.38833	RCAF	**PD497**	I8-K	†
24.02.45	F/O John D. **Flintoft**	Can./ J.37127	RCAF	**PD592**	I8-L	**Eva.**
28.02.45	F/O William R.**Gibbs**	Can./ J.27239	RCAF	**RB338**	I8-K	†
02.03.45	F/L Walter J. **McCarthy**	Can./ J.11325	(us)/RCAF	**MN380**	I8-S	-
24.03.45	F/O Angus M. **Scott**	Can./ J.27239	RCAF	**MN777**	I8-J	-
21.04.45	W/C Frank G. **Grant**	Can./ J.5056	RCAF	**SW452**		-

Total: 55

*Aircraft recovered and repaired, not included in the total

Summary of the aircraft lost by accident - 440 Squadron

Date	*Pilot*	*S/N*	*Origin*	*Serial*	*Code*	*Fate*
18.03.44	P/O Kenneth O. **Mitchell**	Can./ J.19123	RCAF	**JR439**		†
04.05.44	F/O William D. **Peacock**	Can./ J.26271	RCAF	**MN431**	I8-K	†
27.05.44	F/O Nicholas **Stusiak**	Can./ J.35994	RCAF	**MN349**	I8-P	†
03.09.44	F/O Donald C. **Campbell**	Can./ J.28170	RCAF	**MN764**	I8-H	-
08.07.45	F/L Henry T.C. **Taylor**	Can./ J.7432	RCAF	**RB485**	I8-E	-

Total: 5

†

IN MEMORIAM

Hawker Typhoon - The Canadian Squadrons

Name	*Service No*	*Rank*	*Age*	*Origin*	*Date*	*Serial*
AIRSTROP, Charles Sydney	CAN./ J.13484	F/L	24	RCAF	06.10.44	MN805
ALLEN, Ernest James	CAN./ J.20587	F/O	23	RCAF	12.08.44	MN553
ALLMAN, Leonard Ralph	CAN./ J.13588	F/O	24	RCAF	06.06.44	MN428
ANGELINI, Samuel	CAN./ J.37114	F/O	22	RCAF	01.01.45	MN589
ANDERSON, William	CAN./ J.36997	F/O	25	RCAF	24.03.45	MN936
BEIRNES, Jack Rife	CAN./ C.13458	S/L	30	RCAF	01.06.45	SW393
BREEN, Roy Frederick	CAN./ J.92935	P/O	21	RCAF	24.12.44	MP178
BRYDON, Edward Dale	CAN./ J.44042	F/O	21	RCAF	26.04.45	RB429
BUGG, Theodore Alexander	CAN./ J.11316	F/L	22	RCAF	12.08.44	MN687
BURDEN, George Franklin	CAN./ J.88715	F/O	22	RCAF	03.05.45	SW443
BYERS, Harold Noel	CAN./ J.13485	F/L	25	RCAF	23.01.45	RB325
COLEVILLE, John Spencer	CAN./ J.29167	F/O	24	RCAF	18.08.44	MN929
CORDICK, John Morgan	CAN./ J.40775	F/O	25	RCAF	19.11.44	MN801
CORNELISON, John Edgar	CAN./ J.27764	F/O	*n/k*	(US)/RCAF	29.09.44	PD479
CROWLEY, Francis Joseph	CAN./ J.26914	F/O	23	RCAF	11.11.44	MP124
CUMMING, Duncan Herbert	CAN./ J.25086	F/O	23	RCAF	24.12.44	MN665
DAVIS, William George	CAN./ J.29881	F/L	21	RCAF	30.03.45	RB435
DEWAR, John Fraser	CAN./ J.28180	F/O	20	RCAF	12.08.44	MP122
DIXON, Elton Lascelles	CAN./ J.20973	F/O	22	RCAF	20.02.44	R8971
DOIDGE, Ronald William	CAN./ J.26406	F/O	21	RCAF	20.10.44	PD469
DUNKELD, William Thomas	CAN./ J.25085	F/O	23	(US)/RCAF	24.12.44	PD462
ELFNER, Paul James	CAN./ J.22281	F/O	23	RCAF	10.04.44	JR264
GARSIDE, Stanley Vincent	CAN./ J.5068	F/L	24	RCAF	07.06.44	MN548
GIBBS, William Robert	CAN./ J.27239	F/O	21	RCAF	28.02.45	RB338
GOHL, James Garfield	CAN./ J.8356	F/L	24	RCAF	12.06.44	MN115
GRAY, William Alfred	CAN./ J.88900	P/O	23	RCAF	27.09.44	PD458
HARTNETT, Timothy	CAN./ J.91195	F/O	26	(IRE)/RCAF	23.04.45	RB342
HARWOOD, Charles Frederick Joseph	CAN./ J.17954	F/O	25	RCAF	24.12.44	MN453
HICKS, Clifford Waldron	CAN./ J.26912	F/L	22	RCAF	08.08.44	MN313
HILTZ, Robert Arthur	CAN./ J.37855	F/O	20	RCAF	21.11.44	MN124
HOGG, James Easson	CAN./ J.21119	S/L	28	RCAF	23.03.45	MP138
JOHNS, Royce Allen	CAN./ J.21959	F/O	25	RCAF	05.10.44	MN765
KALEN, John	CAN./ J.21856	F/O	21	RCAF	18.07.44	MN574
KEARSE, Percy Harold	CAN./ J.25840	F/O	20	RCAF	21.01.45	PD601
KELLER, Ross Whaley	CAN./ J.37649	F/O	23	RCAF	01.01.45	PD550
KINSELLA, William James	CAN./ J.95521	P/O	22	RCAF	04.04.45	MP181
LAMBERT, Charles Albert	CAN./ J.7827	F/L	25	RCAF	15.12.44	PD478
LAYCOCK, Maurice Preston	CAN./ J.22035	F/O	21	RCAF	28.10.44	MN870
LIPPERT, John William	CAN./ J.27245	F/O	22	RCAF	30.07.44	MN793
LIVINGSTONE, John George Stanley Joseph	CAN./ J.85932	F/O	24	RCAF	14.04.45	MM989
MACDONALD, Ralph Nelson	CAN./ J.21003	F/O	21	RCAF	03.11.44	JR500
MAHAGAN, Wilfred Joseph	CAN./ J.11280	F/L	21	RCAF	07.06.44	MN307
MARTIN, John George	CAN./ J.37648	F/O	23	RCAF	19.11.44	PD607

McAlpine, Earl James	Can./ J.5788	F/L	23	RCAF	04.04.45	RB217
McConvey, Carl Joseph	Can./ J.88446	P/O	23	RCAF	16.07.44	MN770
McCurdy, Roger Eugene George	Can./ J.21517	F/O	23	RCAF	13.08.44	MN720
McKenzie, Robert Melne	Can./ J.11317	F/L	*n/k*	RCAF	18.07.44	MN707
Mitchell, Kenneth Osborne	Can./ J.19123	P/O	22	RCAF	18.03.44	JR439
Moen, Ronald Olaf	Can./ J.22034	F/O	21	RCAF	12.08.44	MN310
Moores, Douglas Keith	Can./ J.17649	F/O	22	RCAF	03.08.44	MN321
Morrison, William Harold	Can./ J.27387	F/O	23	RCAF	15.08.44	MN426
Newsome, Albert Barclay	Can./ J.10652	F/L	27	RCAF	07.10.44	MP135
Park, Lewis E.	Can./ J.12291	F/O	22	(us)/RCAF	27.06.44	MN746
Passmore, Gerald Leroy	Can./ J.35987	F/O	21	RCAF	02.02.45	PD493
Peacock, William Dempsay	Can./ J.26271	F/O	24	RCAF	04.05.44	MN431
Pentland, William Harry	Can./ J.3204	S/L	27	RCAF	07.10.44	MN641
Porrit, Robart Arthur	Can./ J.21202	F/O	21	RCAF	19.08.44	MN401
Reilly, Richard John	Can./ J.38349	F/O	23	RCAF	18.11.44	MN475
Sage, Kenneth Freeland	Can./ C.1191	F/L	24	RCAF	24.12.44	JR506
Saunders, William Lee	Can./ J.22803	F/L	22	RCAF	03.12.44	MN348
Saville, John Walton	Can./ J.8146	F/L	34	RCAF	05.06.44	MN210
Sharpe, George Harold	Can./ J.13612	F/O	22	RCAF	18.08.44	MN347
Scharff, William Kenneth	Can./ J.7814	F/L	25	RCAF	19.08.44	PD448
Schaver, Clarence Lyell	Can./ J.17058	F/L	26	RCAF	02.03.45	MN144
Skelly, Frank Richard Fisher	Can./ J.35985	F/O	24	RCAF	22.01.45	MP128
Stusiak, Nicholas	Can./ J.35984	F/O	24	RCAF	27.05.44	MN349
Sudgen, Alfred William	Can./ J.90713	P/O	25	RCAF	03.12.44	MN251
Swingler, Bernard Percy	Can./ J.21837	F/L	22	RCAF	22.02.45	MP151
Thomas, Frank MacDonald	Can./ J.20648	F/O	21	RCAF	08.07.44	MN464
Vokey, Richard Walter	Can./ J.25397	F/O	21	RCAF	24.09.44	PD465
Wallace, Ivan James Vincent	Can./ J.29904	F/O	25	RCAF	23.01.45	RB333
Warrell, John Francis	Can./ J.38833	F/O	20	RCAF	03.02.45	PD497
Washburn, Dean Jerome	Can./ J.29339	F/O	23	RCAF	24.12.44	MP186
Wilson, Peter	Can./ J.9876	F/L	31	RCAF	01.01.45	PD556
Wright, William Albert	Can./ R.74061	F/Sgt	22	RCAF	24.12.44	PD492

Total: 75

Ireland: 1, Canada: 71, USA: 3

Robert Tremayne Pillsbury Davidson

RAF No. 39968 & Can./ C.89519

Native of Vancouver, Bob Davidson joined the RAF in 1937. Upon his training completed he was posted to the Middle East where he served with 30 Squadron flying Blenheims, first as bombers and then the fighter variant. He moved to Greece in October 1940 where he obtained his initial successes against the Italian aircraft. Subsequently he saw service over the Western Desert after the squadron had re-equipped with Hurricanes. He was now a flight commander. Early in 1942 the unit moved to Ceylon where he made claims over Japanese aircraft and in June 1942 he was given command of 261 Squadron also based in Ceylon but soon tour-expired, he was sent back to the UK in September.

He started a new tour of operations in May 1943 as OC 182 Squadron flying Typhoons, then OC 175 Squadron in July. He led the squadron until September when he was promoted 121 Airfield leader and he was awarded the DFC in October. On 8 January 1944 he made his last claim, and soon after he was transferred to 143 Airfield at the same position. On 8 May he was shot down over France but managed to evade capture joining the French Underground and remained with them until able to reach advancing Allied forces in September. He then returned to the UK but saw no more operational service until the end of the war, being transferred to the RCAF in the meantime in December 1944. He remained with the RCAF after the war.

In April 1944, W/C Davidson received a new Typhoon MN518/R-D. He had six flags painted beneath the windscreen reflecting his scoreboard of two Japanese aircraft, two Italians and two Germans. But it was in a borrowed Typhoon, MM957 of 438, he was lost on 8 May 1944 spending the next four months behind the enemy lines, avoiding capture. *(CT Collection)*

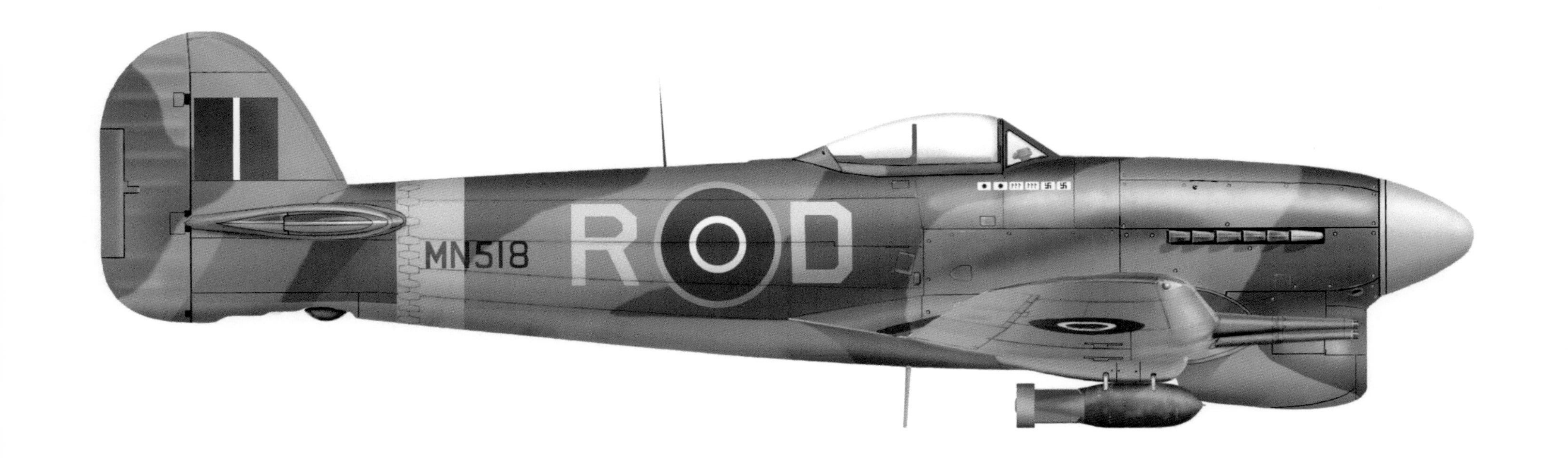

Hawker Typhoon Mk. IB MN518
No. 143 (RCAF) Airfield
Wing Commander Robert T.P. DAVIDSON (Can)
Funtington (UK), April 1944

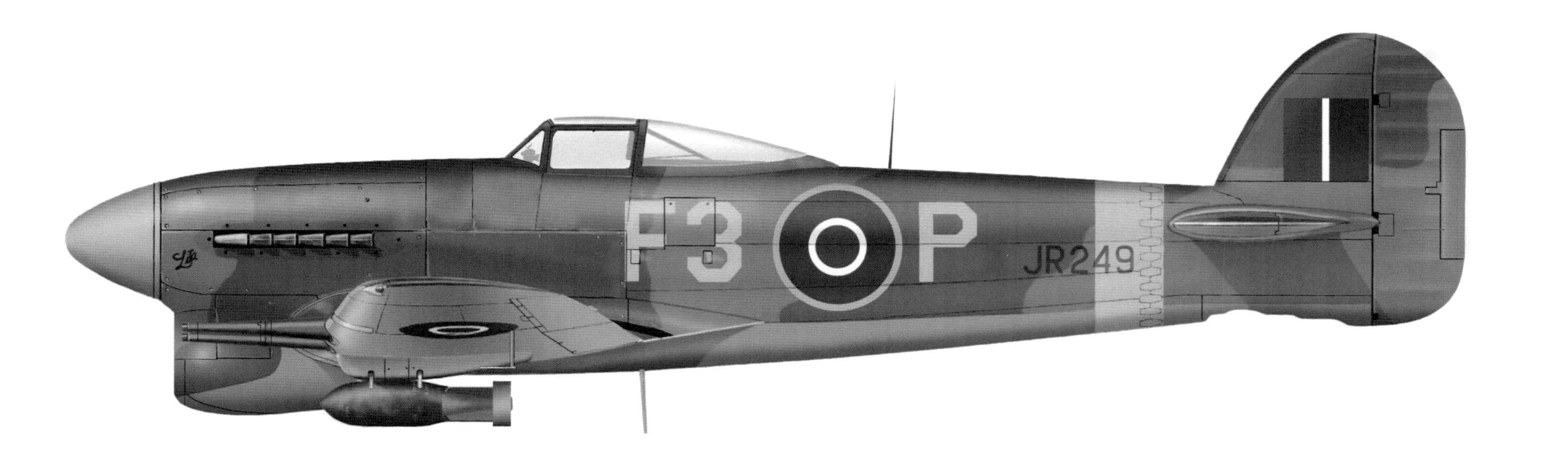

Hawker Typhoon Mk. IB JR249
No. 438 (RCAF) Squadron
Funtington (UK), April 1944

Hawker Typhoon Mk. IB MN716
No. 438 (RCAF) Squadron
B.78/Eindhoven (Netherlands), October 1944

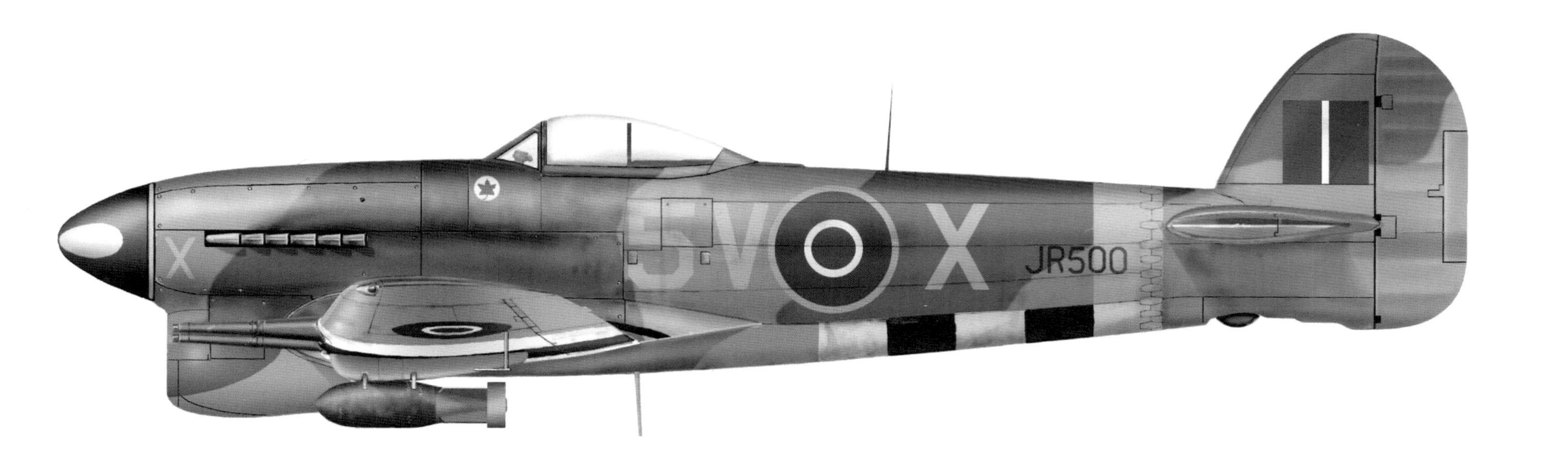

Hawker Typhoon Mk. IB JR500
No. 439 (RCAF) Squadron
B.9/Lantheuil (France), July 1944

Hawker Typhoon Mk. IB RB326
No. 439 (RCAF) Squadron
B.78/Eindhoven (Netherlands), March 1945

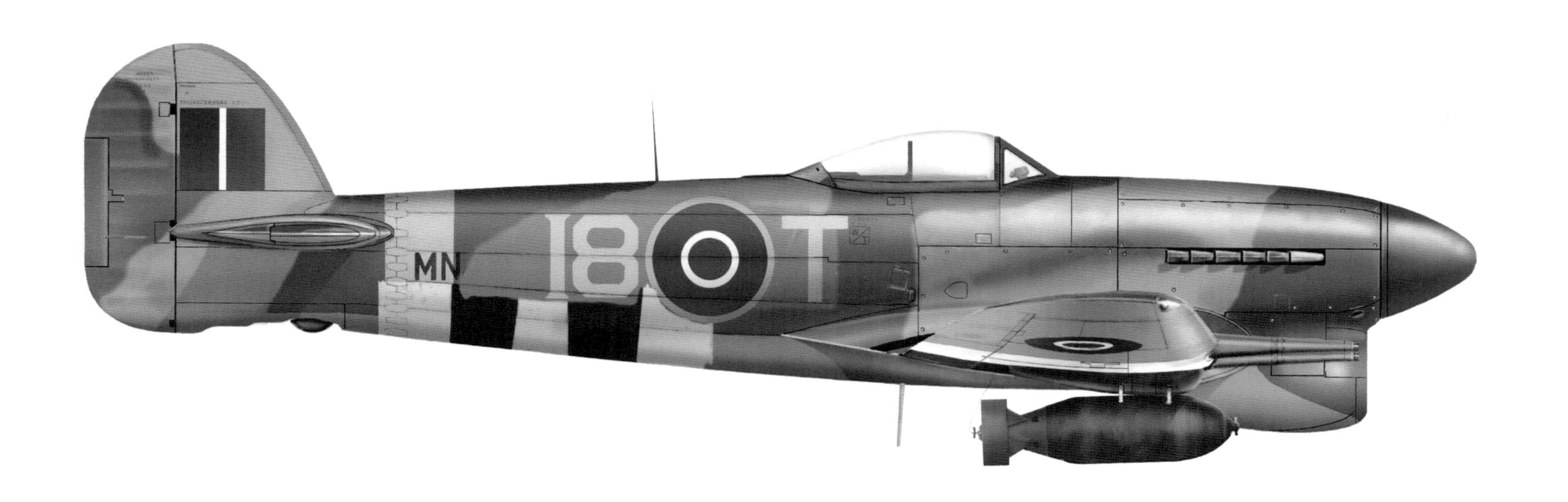

Hawker Typhoon Mk. IB MN413
No. 440 (RCAF) Squadron
B.9/Lantheuil (France), July 1944

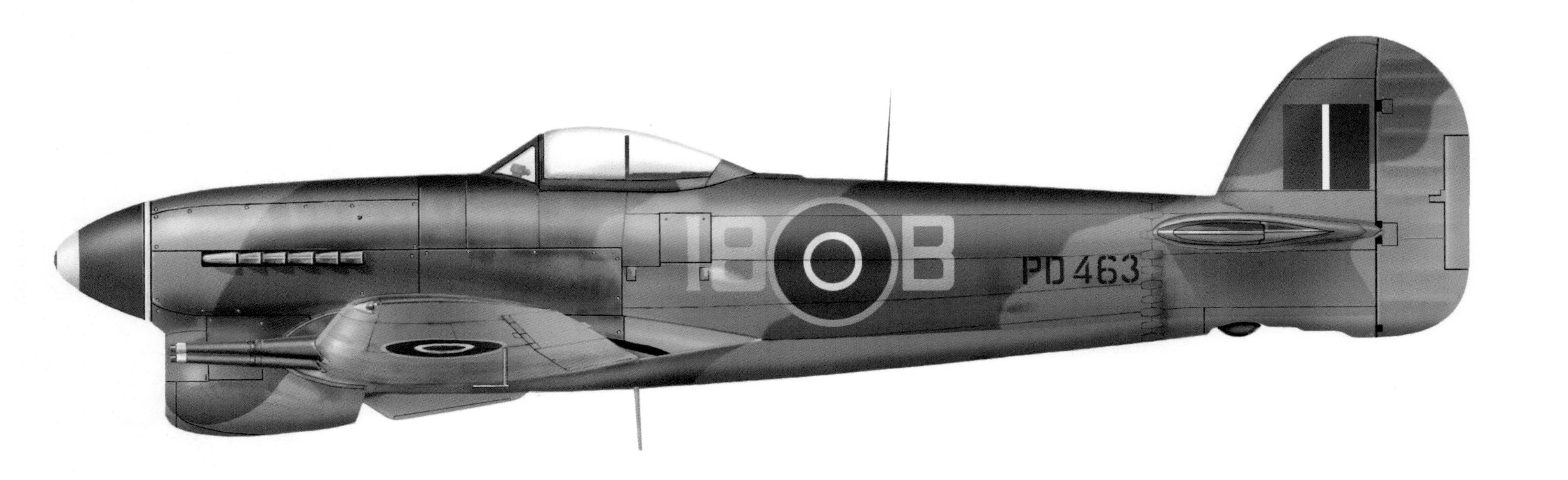

Hawker Typhoon Mk. IB PD463
No. 440 (RCAF) Squadron
B.166/Flensburg (Germany), July 1945

Frank George Grant

CAN./ J.5056

A Canadian from Nova Scotia, Frank Grant enlisted in the RCAF in October 1940. He completed his training in Canada and sailed for the UK in May 1941 with a commission. He attended 56 OTU and was then posted to No. 504 (County of Nottingham) Squadron in August. He became a flight commander in February 1942 but was recalled to Canada the following month where he was posted as a flight commander to No. 118 Squadron RCAF which was transitioning to the Curtiss Kittyhawk. The squadron participated in the Aleutians campaign and Grant took command of the squadron between February and July 1943. After a short rest, he returned to the squadron in November 1943 which was earmarked to serve in Europe under 2 TAF. The squadron was redenominated No. 438 (RCAF) Squadron in February 1944 upon arrival in the UK. It re-equipped with Typhoons and Grant would lead it until the end of July during which the squadron participated in the first phases of the Normandy landings. He was then posted out for a rest. A few weeks before returning to operations, as WingCo Flying of No. 143 (RCAF) Wing in mid-October, he was awarded the DFC. On 24 December 1944, while leading the Wing, he would make his only claim, a Fw190 damaged. He held this position until the following August when he was repatriated to Canada in September 1945 after being awarded the DSO in July. He retired a few days after his return home.

Wing Commander Grant's Typhoon, RB205/FGG seen shortly before it was destroyed on the ground during Operation *Bodenplatte* on 1 January 1945.
(CT Collection)

Hawker Typhoon Mk. IB RB205
No. 143 (RCAF) Wing
Wing Commander Frank G. GRANT (RCAF)
B.78/Eindhoven (Netherlands), December 1944

Typhoon Identity & National Markings 1944/45

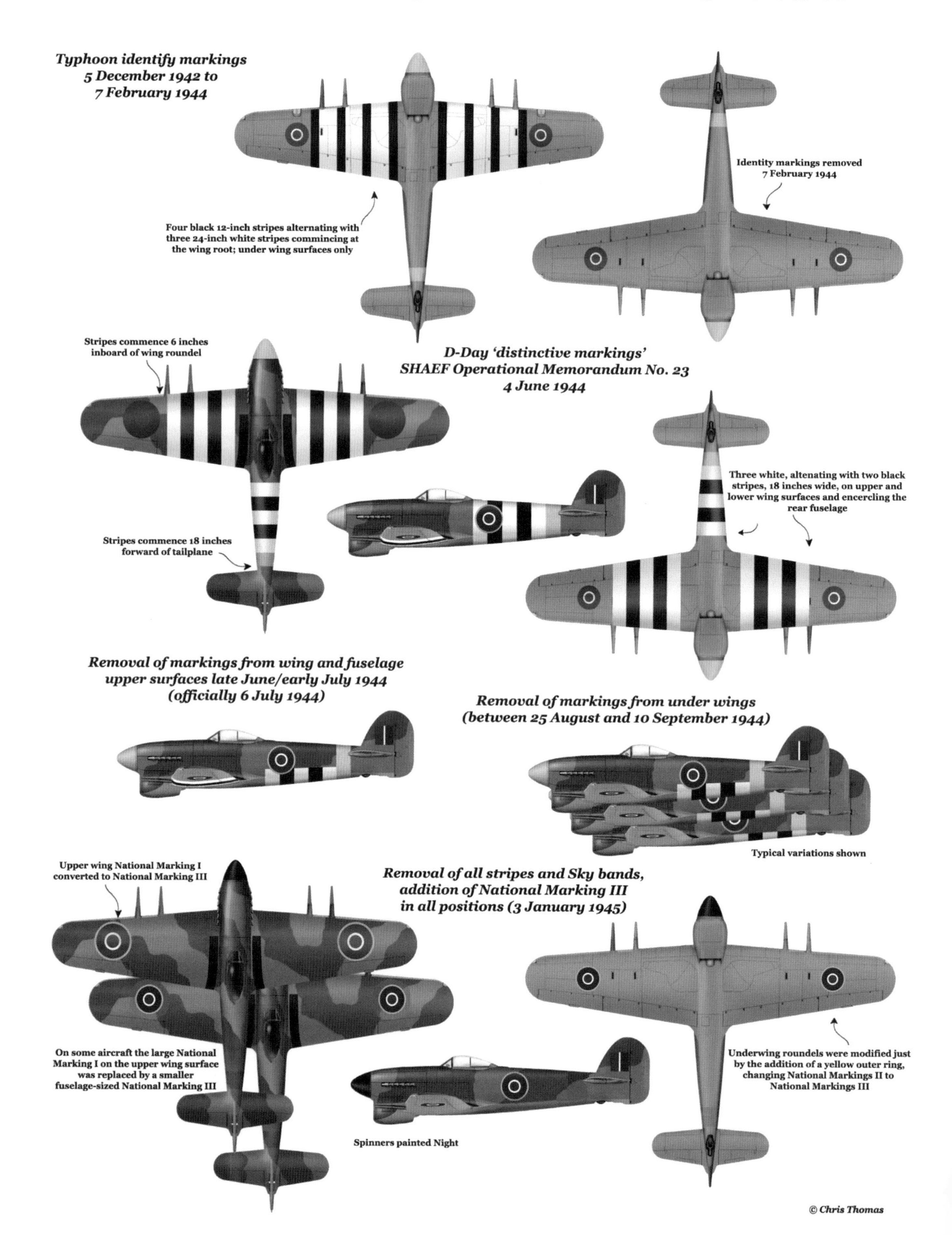

SQUADRONS! - The series

1 The Supermarine Spitfire Mk VI
2 The Republic Thunderbolt Mk I
3 The Supermarine Spitfire Mk V in the Far East
4 The Boeing Fortress Mk I
5 The Supermarine Spitfire Mk XII
6 The Supermarine Spitfire Mk VII
7 The Supermarine Spitfire F. 21
8 The Handley-Page Halifax Mk I
9 The Forgotten Fighters
10 The NA Mustang IV in Western Europe
11 The NA Mustang IV over the Balkans and Italy
12 The Supermarine Spitfire Mk XVI - The British
13 The Martin Marauder Mk I
14 The Supermarine Spitfire Mk VIII in the Southwest Pacific- The British
15 The Gloster Meteor F.I & F.III
16 The NA Mitchell - The Dutch, Poles and French
17 The Curtiss Mohawk
18 The Curtiss Kittyhawk Mk II
19 The Boulton Paul Defiant - day and night fighter
20 The Supermarine Spitfire Mk VIII in the Southwest Pacific - The Australians
21 The Boeing Fortress Mk II & Mk III
22 The Douglas Boston and Havoc - The Australians
23 The Republic Thunderbolt Mk II
24 The Douglas Boston and Havoc - Night fighters
25 The Supermarine Spitfire Mk V - The Eagles
26 The Hawker Hurricane - The Canadians
27 The Supermarine Spitfire Mk V - The 'Bombay' squadrons
28 The Consolidated Liberator - The Australians
29 The Supermarine Spitfire Mk XVI - The Dominions
30 The Supermarine Spitfire Mk V - The Belgian and Dutch squadrons
31 The Supermarine Spitfire Mk V - The New Zealanders
32 The Supermarine Spitfire Mk V - The Norwegians
33 The Brewster Buffalo
34 The Supermarine Spitfire Mk II - The Foreign squadrons
35 The Martin Marauder Mk II
36 The Supermarine Spitfire Mk V - The Special Reserve squadrons
37 The Supermarine Spitfire Mk XIV - The Belgian and Dutch squadrons
38 The Supermarine Spitfire Mk II - The Rhodesian, Dominion & Eagle squadrons
39 The Douglas Boston and Havoc - Intruders
40 The North American Mustang Mk III over Italy and the Balkans (Pt-1)
41 The Bristol Brigand
42 The Supermarine Spitfire Mk V - The Australians
43 The Hawker Typhoon - The Rhodesian squadrons
44 The Supermarine Spitfire F.22 & F.24
45 The Supermarine Spitfire Mk IX - The Belgian and Dutch squadrons
46 The North American & CAC Mustang - The RAAF
47 The Westland Whirlwind
48 The Supermarine Spitfire Mk XIV - The British squadrons
49 The Supermarine Spitfire Mk I - The beginning (the Auxiliary squadrons)
50 The Hawker Tempest Mk V - The New Zealanders
51 The Last of the Long-Range Biplane Flying Boats
52 The Supermarine Spitfire Mk IX - The Former Canadian Homefront squadrons
53 The Hawker Hurricane Mk I & Mk II - The Eagle squadrons
54 The Hawker biplane fighters
55 The Supermarine Spitfire Mk IX - The Auxiliary squadrons
56 The Hawker Typhoon - The Canadian squadrons

USN AIRCRAFT 1922-1962
Vol.7: Type Designation Letter 'F' (Pt-4)
Phil H. LISTEMANN
RAF, DOMINION & ALLIED SQUADRONS AT WAR: STUDY, HISTORY AND STATISTICS
No.137 Squadron 1941 - 1945
COMPILED BY
PHIL H. LISTEMANN WITH CHRIS THOMAS
No.3
The Supermarine
in the Far East
Fighter Leaders
Volume VII
No.10
Mustang Mk. IV
in Western Europe
www.RAF-IN-COMBAT.com
- USN Aircraft 1922-1962 -
- Squadrons! -
- RAF, Dominion and Allied squadrons at War -
- Allied Wings -
- Famous squadrons of WW2 -
- Fighter Leaders -
RAF, DOMINION & ALLIED SQUADRON AT WAR: STUDY, HISTORY AND STATISTICS
1941 - 1945
No.453 (R.A.A.F.) Squadron
1941-1945
ALLIED WINGS
The Bristol
Brigand

Printed in Great Britain
by Amazon